This book discusses two approaches available to firms to adopt successful circular strategies: Circular Networks and Circular Districts. The former, focusing my approach considers [illegible] challenges [illegible] business models into practice [illegible] discusses [illegible] vehicles to [illegible] strategies by considering [illegible] principles. The book highlights how firms should [illegible] strategy, [illegible] networks of relationships, and [illegible] process when circular economy is a concrete [illegible] book explores the circular [illegible] circular economy [illegible] the motivations [illegible] from firms and supply chains [illegible] strategies by taking the circular district perspective. The latter plays a new role within modern economy systems and this book conceptualizes and operationalizes its definition. The circular district can represent an effective way to accelerate the energy transition [illegible] developing [illegible] and exploiting [illegible]

[illegible]

[illegible] Chair [illegible] NOVA [illegible] International Journal of Production [illegible]

Pierroberto [illegible] Professor [illegible] School of Management at [illegible] Paris, in 2008 [illegible] as well as an Adjunct Professor in Management of Circular [illegible] Department of [illegible] Management. With a particular attention for the human capital and the creation of strong team working, Pierroberto has been CEO of [illegible] years. Being a great supporter of innovation and [illegible] he is involved in several programs on analyzing and selecting [illegible] with a specific focus on innovative ideas, new business models, and promotion of young talents. Since May 2017, he is CEO and Managing Director of the [illegible] Group, one of the [illegible] national firms in the [illegible] sector.

Strategies for the Circular Economy

Circular Districts and Networks

Pietro De Giovanni
Pierroberto Folgiero

Strategies for the Circular Economy

Circular Districts and Networks

Routledge
Taylor & Francis Group
LONDON AND NEW YORK

G. Giappichelli Editore

First published 2023
by Routledge
4 Park Square, Milton Park, Abingdon, Oxon OX14 4RN

and by Routledge
605 Third Avenue, New York, NY 10158

Routledge is an imprint of the Taylor & Francis Group, an informa business

and by G. Giappichelli Editore
Via Po 21, Torino – Italia

British Library Cataloguing-in-Publication Data
A catalogue record for this book is available from the British Library

ISBN: 978-1-032-45817-5 (hbk-Routledge)
ISBN: 978-1-003-37884-6 (ebk-Routledge)
ISBN: 978-1-032-45819-9 (pbk-Routledge)
ISBN: 978-88-921-2378-6 (hbk-Giappichelli)

Typeset in Simoncini Garamond
by G. Giappichelli Editore, Turin, Italy

The manuscript has been subjected to a peer review process prior to publication.

CONTENTS

LIST OF FIGURES AND TABLES

Tables

Part I – Chapter 3

Part I – Chapter 4

Part II – Chapter 1

Part II – Chapter 2

PREFACE

The circular economy has recently received considerable attention, as it represents an effective and valid option for aligning production systems and sustainable strategies with worldwide environmental and social objectives. The circular economy allows businesses to create efficient reverse system solutions by adopting the principles of reduce, reuse, and recycle, as described in the well-known waste pyramid proposed by the Ellen McCarthy Foundation. Although several circular economy systems models and frameworks have been built upon the original waste pyramid, new emerging mega trends like sophistication of products and consumers' needs, digital transformation, Covid-19 outbreaks, worldwide raw material shortages, international crises, and global warming impose urgent and comprehensive updates of those models and frameworks with new ingredients.

This book seeks to achieve such goals by proposing a new and original learning path, starting from an analysis of the strategies available for firms and policy makers relative to circular economy systems and develops a circular economy cascade, which is an evolution of the traditional waste pyramid model. Next, the book proposes the concept of circular districts to the scientific community and the business world and applies the related framework to case studies and practical applications. Therefore, this book allows professionals, executives, and business leaders to gain fresh and original knowledge about various aspects of circular economy systems, including: selecting and implementing the right circular economy strategies, evaluating the available public mechanisms to support circular economy projects and appropriate of the highest possible value, identifying the proper circular network to put a circular economy into execution, understanding the role of digital technologies to shift from traditional to smart circular economy systems, and realizing the opportunities that both firms and policy makers have when sponsoring the implementation of circular districts.

Considering that this book contains new strategic developments in the circular economy area, it allows scholars and Ph.D. students to identify new research avenues and possible future projects in the field. Furthermore, the book provides inspiration for managers, practitioners, and policy makers to develop modern circular economy systems by properly evaluating and including all applicable business ingredients. Finally, this book perfectly fits with graduate and post-graduate program content, thereby allowing students to recognize the best paths to properly integrate the circular economy within corporate and functional strategies.

As mentioned, this book focuses on two approaches available to firms to shape successful circular strategies: circular economy cascade and circular districts. Hence, the book is organized into 3 parts and 8 chapters in total, through which readers will become acquainted with the critical aspects, driving factors, opportunities, and challenges linked to these two paradigms.

The first part comprises 5 chapters. Chapter 1 provides an analysis of the circular economy strategies and proposes an evolution of the traditional waste pyramid with the circular economy cascade. The latter includes an evaluation of both the product life cycle and the returns' residual value to select the proper circular economy strategy. Chapter 2 makes a comprehensive analysis of the stakeholders interacting in circular economy systems, including firms, supply chains, consumers, policy makers, institutions, and governments. It explores the critical criteria for selecting the right stakeholders and implementing the most efficient and effective circular economy networks. Chapter 3 proposes a link between the circular economy strategies and the public mechanisms available to support its implementation and management to enable circular economy projects to be pursued even when the related output is not economically appealing. Chapter 4 analyzes the strategic options that firms have to appropriate of the economic value inherent a circular economy framework, also using recent technologies like blockchain. Chapter 5 crosses traditional circular economy systems with new mega trends like digital transformation, smart cities, and omnichannel strategies; hence, this chapter derives fresh ideas and insights to rethink traditional circular economy systems and reinvent the business models accordingly.

The second part of this book comprises one chapter that explores the business and entrepreneurial potential linked to the shift from the circular economy thinking to the green circular districts thinking. It shows how circular districts can be an effective option for the worldwide energy transition by developing and using green technologies and clean solutions. Therefore, this chapter opens the discussion around the creation of green circular districts and leaves tools with which readers can evaluate both the economic and environmental feasibility of such projects.

Finally, the book ends with the third part, which comprises two chapters giving details on two business cases that apply the new concepts and paradigms proposed throughout the book, specifically circular economy cascade and green circular districts.

Overall, this work analyses the circular economy approaches by discussing both the opportunities and the difficulties that firms face in reshaping the corporate strategies by considering circular economy principles using modern and original frameworks. The evolution from circular economy to circular districts reveals the motivation to redesign circular economy systems by taking a district perspective, including green technology advancements and progresses, as well as atypical business models and new industrial collaborations.

September, 2022
Rome

Pietro De Giovanni
Professor of Circular Economy,
International Operations and
Supply Chain

Part I

Chapter 1
CIRCULAR ECONOMY STRATEGIES AND APPROACHES

Pietro De Giovanni

ABSTRACT: *This chapter introduces the links between the circular economy and waste pyramid to develop the waste cascade and identify the strategies and practices that firms can adopt to implement a successful circular system. Among the various blocks of the waste cascade, the chapter focuses on "Reduction, Reuse, and Recycling", as those have a direct and strategic link to circular economy. Within each of these blocks, the chapter offers genuine insights on how circular economy can reshape the firms' strategies and provide an original source of business opportunities.*

1.1. Circular economy and the waste cascade

The current debate on the circular economy involving the scientific community, institutions, and business has become very popular due to the fantastic opportunities that it offers as well as today's emerging challenges in terms of environmental restrictions and global warming. The circular economy emerges as a new paradigm for firms and countries to promote the diffusion of new production models and sustainable consumption behaviors. In fact, the circular economy assumes a shift from a linear economy to a circular one that is guaranteed through both process and product innovations followed by new marketing strategies and organizational structures.

The literature has identified the circular economy within the triple "reduction, reuse, and recycle" concepts, which are key ingredients of the new strategic paradigm. The need to adopt a circular economy model is linked to the principles of environmental sustainability, social inclusion, and business convenience. Therefore, the circular economy requires a high level of knowledge that involves multiple stakeholders and that seeks to optimize various aspects of business at the same time. By focusing on reduction, reuse, and recycle, the new production models move away from traditional linear systems that are mostly based on cost reduction and product differentiation with a focus on the forward activities that create value for customers and for society at large. These targets, which are indeed fully valid and have the merit to be part of the corporate strategy, require the adoption of circular systems that incorporate backward flows and integrate them with traditional forward activities.

According to the Ellen MacArthur Foundation (2015), the circular economy paradigm identifies traditional production and business models by sponsoring the rational management of resources and finding new paths for the creation of value, also including social and environmental spheres [1]. Hence, the circular economy literature [2] has developed the triple "reduction, reuse, and recycle" paradigm as follows:

- Reduction: This principle is highly inspired by the traditional industrial paradigms of mass production and lean production that were based on efficiency linked to different drivers. Applied to the circular economy, the principle of efficiency it is based on the minimization of inputs to pursue a minimal utilization of virgin raw materials while using and appropriating the residual value of waste and returns.
- Reuse: Some of the components that return back through the backward flows can be directly reused to make either new products or refurbished products. When firms invest in product reusability, the circular economy aims at extending their product lifecycle.
- Recycling: The principle of recycling links to firms' capability to recover material from waste and inject them into production processes. The circular economy approach can then include recycling operations to reacquire the traditional properties of a product or to use the recycling material for other types of applications.

In waste management, reduction, reuse, and recycling are the blocks of the waste management pyramid [3], which is elaborated in the *waste cascade* in Figure 1. The figure indicates an order of actions to identify and construct a sustainable strategy by showing the stages of waste management to be undertaken according to sustainability targets, product value, usage opportunities, and product lifecycle. Therefore, the waste cascade guides toward a sustainable strategy by obtaining the maximum value from products

[1] MacArthur, E., Zumwinkel, K., & Stuchtey, M.R. (2015). Growth within: A circular economy vision for a competitive Europe. Ellen MacArthur Foundation.

[2] Ghisellini, P., Cialani, C., & Ulgiati, S. (2016). A review on circular economy: The expected transition to a balanced interplay of environmental and economic systems. *Journal of Cleaner Production*, *114*, 11-32.

[3] Carter, C.R., & Ellram, L.M. (1998). Reverse logistics: A review of the literature and framework for future investigation. *Journal of Business Logistics*, *19*(1), 85.

while reducing the amount of waste in the lifecycle and optimizing the circular economy practices through the analysis of possible usages. Within the cascade, the blocks for reduction, reuse, and recycle directly link to the implementation of circular economy systems, while the others require the implementation of other types of sustainable practices and strategies.

Figure 1. The waste cascade.

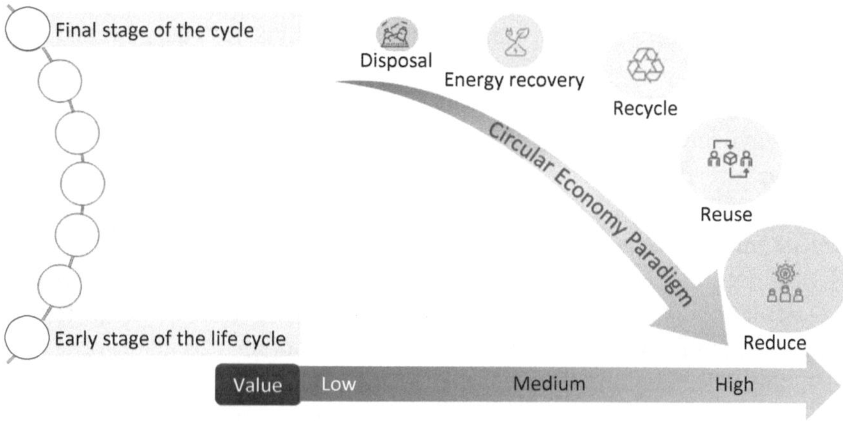

1.2. The "Reduction" principle

Reduction is linked to the concept of eco-efficiency, which basically signifies "doing more with less" [4]. In fact, eco-efficiency is linked to the concept of creating more goods and services while using fewer resources and creating less waste and pollution [5]. In this sense, the circular economy can be very beneficial by reducing the amount of natural resources consumed; decreasing energy use, emissions, and waste by cutting the amount of toxic waste created or emitted; and decreasing the amount of virgin materials to be used. To be effective, eco-efficiency should be measured. Several indicators have been proposed for this purpose in the past, like utilization and consumption. Specifically, some indicators are the domestic extraction of raw materials comparative to the demand and the reduction of water con-

---

[4] McDonough, W., & Braungart, M. (2010). *Cradle to cradle: Remaking the way we make things*. North point press.

[5] Yu, Y., Chen, D., Zhu, B., & Hu, S. (2013). Eco-efficiency trends in China, 1978-2010: Decoupling environmental pressure from economic growth. *Ecological Indicators*, *24*, 177-184.

sumption by changing the production processes. Therefore, the reaction-related eco-efficiency that firms are able to reach leads to sustainable development, which requires indicators expressed in ratios and linked to internal and external resources, the product lifecycles, and the performance of logistics and procurement as well as indicators linked to input consumption and natural resource utilization. Cabeza et al. (2013) reviewed the low carbon and low energy consumption material in the building sector[6]. According to their review, the energy performance of a building depends on the energy spent in making the materials rather than the energy consumption of the building *per se* during the lifecycle. In this sense, the analysis of eco-efficiency requires two major ingredients: The economic value added and the environmental impact. According to Gavrilescu (2004), the best way to capture the economic value created is represented by the net present value (NPV) and the internal rate of return (IRR)[7]. Furthermore, the environmental impact can be measured according to the abiotic resources depletion potential (ADP), the global warming potential (GWP), the ozone layer depletion potential (ODP), photochemical oxidation potential (POCP), human toxicity potential (HTP), ecological toxicity potential (ETP), the acidification potential (AP), and the eutrophication potential (EP). Then, the eco-efficiency can be computed according to two indicators:

$$Economic\ Added\ Value = \frac{Market\ value\ of\ products}{Cost\ of\ raw\ material\ and\ energy}$$

$$Environmental\ Impact\ Ratio = \frac{Environmental\ impact}{Environmental\ credits}$$

The Economic Added Value informs on the value that a firm obtains when selling products in comparison to the cost of inputs (e.g., raw material, energy). In contrast, the Environmental Impact Ratio informs on the negative impact that products have to the environment in comparison to the benefits obtainable from the circular economy. Then, the eco-efficiency can be computed as:

$$Eco-efficiency\ indicator = \frac{Economic\ Added\ Value}{Environmental\ Impact\ Ratio}$$

[6] Cabeza, L.F., Barreneche, C., Miró, L., Morera, J.M., Bartolí, E., & Fernández, A.I. (2013). Low carbon and low embodied energy materials in buildings: A review. *Renewable and Sustainable Energy Reviews*, *23*, 536-542.

[7] Gavrilescu, M. (2014). Biorefinery systems: An overview. Bioenergy Research: Advances and Applications. 1, 219-241.

The eco-efficiency indicator reflects the earlier mentioned definition "doing more with less", which can be obtained, for example, by reducing the cost of raw materials or the environmental impact.

1.3. The "Reuse" principle for materials

The *Reuse* principle refers to materials when the collected outcomes are perceived – in many instances – as waste to get rid of. In fact, the materials do not necessarily have any residual value for consumers though they take up capacity and capabilities of firms. Instead, materials can be reused by extending their purposes for the same types of applications or assigning them for alternative application and use. The main challenge that customers must face is recognizing the benefits of reusing some materials for different industries and sectors. The use of materials, which is different from recycling (which we will come back to later), refers to handling materials with the purpose of diverting them from a waste stream. Reusers, therefore, keep materials out of waste by either avoiding processing them or making negligible production steps. The use of materials is then linked to several collection programs that can bring various benefits. First, environmental benefits can be observed in terms of fewer resources, energy, and labor compared to other tasks like recycling; benefits are also linked to the local community, since society at large needs materials for people's basic needs such as food, buildings, and clothing. Furthermore, reusing materials instead of using virgin materials means there is less burden on economic systems as a whole.

According to Sherman (2019), the reuse principle requires connecting the circular economy to two types of sustainable operations: The physical space (warehouse or storefront) to store the materials and products available for reuse as well as brokering and listing the related services[8]. In fact, these two sustainable operations have been highly successful in the United States for many years by leading to the following collection options for material waste:

- Industrial materials exchange services. Waste exchange programs can be linked to the reuse principle for both material and goods; it consists of a platform for firms, even across different industries, on which reusable "waste" can be exchanged with other firms that can use those items or materials for their industrial purposes. Therefore, the platforms of

[8] Sherman, R. (2019). Before You Recycle, Choose to Reuse, NC State Extension Publications, Sept. 18th.

these types of programs must be populated with information on available waste and surplus of materials, which can be visible to other firms through social media and interaction points like newsletters, webpages, and catalogues. The firms can either contact and exchange with each other directly or formalize the circularity through an exchange service.
- Individual materials exchanges. In North Carolina, local governments have acquired competences in managing ad hoc waste material to be reused, such as paint or pallets, and operate them on a continuous basis.

According to Sherman (2019), the materials listed in waste exchanges typically include the following items: Acids and alkalis, construction materials, containers and pallets, discontinued products, durables and electronics, glass, metals and metal sludge, oil and wax, other inorganic and organic chemicals, paint and coatings, plastic and rubber, solvents, surplus equipment, textiles and leather, unused supplies, and wood and paper.

Indeed, the analysis of the materials to be reused depends on the sector from which the materials are collected. As an example, Blander (2019) made a comprehensive analysis of the materials that can be collected through the circular economy and be reused for further applications in the construction industry[9]. The analysis started by selecting the materials and distinguishing between reusable materials and recyclable materials. The sorting tasks that were carried out to make such a distinction led to valuable and well-identifiable outcomes of circular economy systems. Accordingly, the materials in the building and construction sector can be considered within that circular economy system and must be carefully evaluated and classified. Among them, the most important material waste that can be reused are:

- **Drywall.** Drywall is a very complicated material since it can be contaminated with other materials and substances, which make it not properly usable or easy to treat. However, being able to collect the drywall material in good enough condition allows construction companies to fully reuse it.
- **Wood.** Wood is one of the most frequently reused materials in the construction industry, since its structure is unaltered even after a demolition. Therefore, instead of considering it as a waste material to be disposed of, wood can be reused to make floors and furniture. Generally speaking, wood collected from the circular economy of the construction industry is in good condition, although it may require some processing when it is used as composite materials.

[9] Blander, A. (2019). When a building comes down, where do its materials go? Metropolis. https://metropolismag.com/viewpoints/recycling-demolition-building-materials/.

- **Plastic.** Buildings and their construction require a high quantity of plastic that can be found in different parts, like in packaging or piping. Indeed, as with other industrial applications, the plastic collected from the construction industry can offer several opportunities. For example, plastic materials can be reused for packaging or in landscaping, making new drainage pipes, or floor ducts and flooring.
- **Aggregate.** The aggregate coming from the circular economy system of the construction sector can be used either for recycling—a compacted mass of fragments or particles—or for reuse purposes like making concrete or as backfill material. Surely, the aggregate material from the construction industry should never be sent to landfills.
- **Glass.** The construction industry is characterized by a high amount of glass material that is obtained by the circular economy activities on a certain site. The material can be fully reused after some processing due to its fragility; however, glass material is almost guaranteed to be fully reusable. Rather than only focusing on the traditional applications of glass material, construction companies can use it also to manufacture bricks, aggregate, and as decoration material. Although the properties that make glass material very appealing as a subject in circular economy systems, collecting and recovering glass can be an expensive process, especially when it is contaminated and requires atypical processing before being treated and reused.
- **Insulation.** The circular economy in the construction sector allows for collecting a lot of material for insulation, which is highly reusable. Examples of insulation material reuse are the simple reuse of the off-cuts and the removal of possible contaminants like nails. While the possible reuse applications are feasible, the circular process behind it could be more expensive than the insulation material itself, which is cheap when purchased as a virgin material. Furthermore, the insulation material is exposed to a high risk of contamination, making the restoring process very expensive.
- **Other possibilities.** Other types of construction materials can also be collected through the circular economy. For example, steel is also present when demolishing buildings and can be used as a waste material for reinforcing the infrastructure of new buildings. Furthermore, the concrete resulting from a demolition can be reused to make new pavement, while untreated timber can be used as mulch for improving both soil moisture and fertility.

This example of the construction industry gives a deep reflection on the heterogeneity that waste materials have even when coming from the same source (e.g., demolishing a building). The managerial challenge that firms face consists of implementing and coordinating circular economy systems that are able to manage these material types simultaneously, though each material has its own peculiarities and characteristics and might require special treatments. Hence, the increasing complexity of material waste will make the implementation and the optimization of a circular economy extremely difficult and challenging.

1.4. The "Reuse" principle for goods

Whenever the "Reuse" principle refers to goods, society at large should be reengineered to identify the best methods and the principal actors involved in that process. Within local communities, various forms of informal collections take place, where people can make their used products available to other social clusters (e.g., the collection of clothes for charity) or simply making them available to everyone. It is common to see waste collection points and/or drop-off points managed by volunteers who promote the reuse of products that still have a residual value. Society at large needs a certain capacity to accommodate and manage circular economy systems. Relative to the reuse principle linked to products, the following collection options can be identified [10]:

- Swap shops. Swap shops have been engineered with the purpose of collecting "things" that people would have normally discarded and making them available to others at little or no cost. Swap shops can be created and managed either by firms or by local authorities. In the former, they are designed as areas that collect any type of materials and products, also acting through differentiated waste. In the latter, local authorities and governments set up swap shops at landfills or collection centers to let the public drop off non-hazardous reusable items and also pick up things they can use.
- Surplus stores. Surplus stores accept items that have reached their end-of-use stage, like furniture and office equipment, and make them available to the public either for free or for small amounts. In most cases, *surplus* stores are operated by large and public institutions such as universities. However, surplus stores can be also managed by the government at a high level by providing used equipment, vehicles, and supplies for public institutions and local governments.
- Scrap exchanges. Scrap exchanges accept industrial scrap or printer overruns and distribute them for free or sell them at a nominal cost to

[10] Sherman R. (2019). *Ibidem*.

schools, day-care centers, senior centers, and nonprofit organizations with arts programming. The scrap materials can be used in art and drama classes and in a variety of arts and crafts programs. Schools and other organizations can contact businesses directly to obtain scrap materials or they can use a scrap exchange.

– Secondhand stores. In many countries, the circular economy made by secondhand stores is very common. These collection options can be either private or non-profit organizations that can target specific social outcomes, like gathering donations for local schools and hospitals, or manage the collection of secondhand goods in a more traditional way, according to people's voluntary actions and ethical behaviors. In this sense, secondhand stores are not classical waste reduction options but rather outlets for products that can be reused instead of discarded.

The physical platforms identified by Sherman (2019) have been followed and complemented by digital transformation processes and have opened the way for sharing economy options in this direction. In fact, sharing economy platforms provide a peer-to-peer means for connecting secondhand product users with the providers. According to Belk (2014), "Sharing is a phenomenon as old as humankind, while collaborative consumption and the sharing economy are phenomena born of the Internet age" [11]. This emerging trend is possible thanks to digital technologies as well as innovative corporate strategies and business models through which collaborative consumption becomes possible and is exemplified by using online platforms for obtaining, giving, and sharing access to goods and services. Furthermore, sharing can happen by either giving access through ownership or by transferring ownership, which happens through swapping, donations, or purchasing used goods [12]. Therefore, the circular economy definitely depends on the collaborative intentions on the sharing platforms, which leads to continuous contributions and heavy use of the platforms' resources. Ek Styvén and Mariani (2020) undertook both supply-side and demand-side perspectives when identifying the proper sharing economy option for used products and argued the existence of three drivers helping to adopt the best peer-to-peer platform [13], specifically: 1. Technology:

---

[11] Belk, R. (2014). You are what you can access: Sharing and collaborative consumption online. *Journal of Business Research*, *67*(8), 1595-1600.

[12] Hamari, J., Sjöklint, M., & Ukkonen, A. (2016). The sharing economy: Why people participate in collaborative consumption. *Journal of the Association for Information Science and Technology*, *67*(9), 2047-2059.

[13] Ek Styvén, M., & Mariani, M.M. (2020). Understanding the intention to buy

Technological advancement, mostly through the development of digital technologies, the Internet, online services, and digital platforms, allow society at large to rent, lend, swap, donate, or purchase used goods; 2. Supply of used products: A market for used products can exist if there is an industry for it and related competition along with a network of consumers that supports the supply-side and creates the structure; 3. Social and psychological drivers: A project based on the circular economy for used products starts from the analysis of social and psychological factors that push and drive people to interact on sharing platforms and underpinning unconventional behaviors like lending and renting mechanisms or transferring of ownership through swapping, donating, or purchasing used goods. These factors represent both the antecedents and the drivers of any circular economy system based on used products.

1.5. The "Recycling" principle

"Recycling" is the process of collecting and processing materials that would otherwise be thrown away as trash and turning them into new products. Firms adopting recycling must have the facilities and capabilities to completely destroy the collected products and convert them into materials to be used in production. From a biological perspective, a substance is available for recycling after the natural processes of biochemical degradation or modification to regain material for human activities.

The recycling principle has gained popularity all over the world, since governments have imposed important restrictions through legislation for sustainable and circular economy strategies as well as for the treatments involved in the various recycling steps. For example, the EU Directive 2000/53/EC [14] set the recycling rates to be reached for passenger vehicles. Since 2015, for all end-of-life vehicles, the reuse and recycling must increase by 85% according to the average weight per vehicle and year. Similarly, in the textile industry, the EU Directive 2008/98/EC [15] regulates recycling activities, since textile waste is considered to be special waste and therefore needs special treatment. This restriction impacts firms' plans and strategies, as they are directed to use a specific disposal system depending on the level of disassembly of the recovered materials. According to Sandin

secondhand clothing on sharing economy platforms: The influence of sustainability, distance from the consumption system, and economic motivations. *Psychology & Marketing, 37*(5), 724-739.

[14] https://eur-lex.europa.eu/legal-content/EN/ALL/?uri=celex%3A32000L0053.

[15] https://eur-lex.europa.eu/legal-content/EN/TXT/?uri=celex%3A32008L0098.

and Peters (2018), if the fabric of a textile product is recovered and reused in new products, it is classified as *fabric recycling*[16]. If the fabric is dissembled, but the original fibers are preserved, then the textile is classified as *fibre recycling*. If the fibers are dissembled but the polymers or oligomers are preserved, it is *polymer/oligomer recycling*. If the polymers/oligomers are dissembled but the monomers are preserved, this is *monomer recycling*. Indeed, the recycling costs associated with this classification can vary substantially, since the recycling process requires a combination of various mechanical, chemical, and thermal processes.

While it is out of the scope of this work to review all EU Directives in the theme of recycling restrictions, it is important to consider the difference between the recycling potential and the recycling rate. The former refers to the amount of material that can be potentially subject to recycling and that provides opportunities to be evaluated in such directions. The latter measures the quantity of recyclable material that can be recycled, with considerations for technological advancements, economic convenience, and possible environmental impacts. According to van Schaik and Reuter (2004), passenger vehicles are subject to a high recycling rate[17]. For example, the metal content of cars can be fully recovered, providing a potential recycling of 100%; however, the recycling rate is much lower than that, since the quality of the recycled material results from a mechanical separation process that depends on thermodynamics and kinetics processes. Furthermore, the increased complexity of recycling pyrometallurgy and the current composition of vehicles containing a combination of metals considerably decreases the recycling rate.

[16] Sandin, G., & Peters, G.M. (2018). Environmental impact of textile reuse and recycling. A review. *Journal of Cleaner Production*, *184*, 353-365.

[17] Van Schaik, A., & Reuter, M.A. (2004). The time-varying factors influencing the recycling rate of products. *Resources, Conservation and Recycling*, *40*(4), 301-328.

Figure 2. Forward and backward flow analysis.

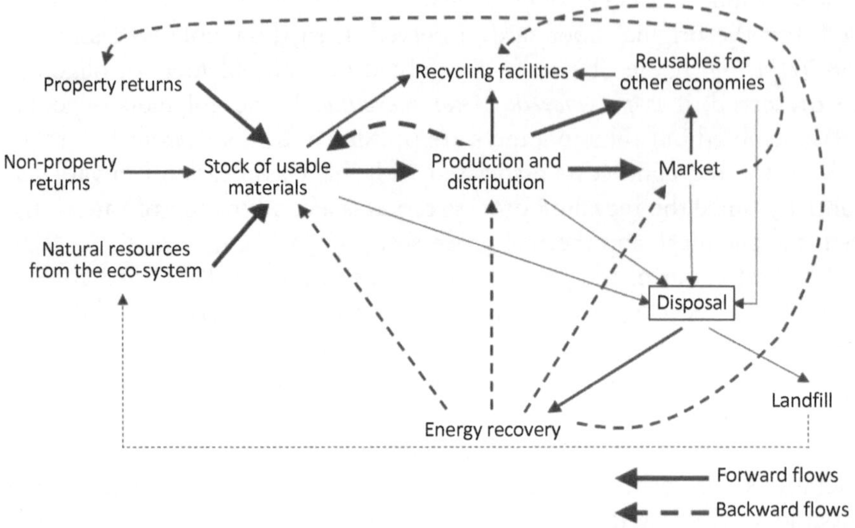

To consider the complexity of recycling, Haas et al. (2015) assessed the circular economy potential by analyzing the material flows, waste production, and recycling rates within one unique framework [18], which is reproposed in Figure 2 according to the waste cascade. The theoretical framework proposed in the figure illustrates how the material flow is considered at a global level and how the processes used to properly treat them can be quantified within a circular economy setting. The latter is based on a model applied to an economy-wide material flow accounting proposed by Eurostat [19], which defines the flow of materials from extraction and import, by processing, immediate consumption, or temporary accumulation in material stocks to recycling or final treatment before all materials leave the system as waste and emissions. To assess the circularity of an economy based on the material flows, Haas et al. (2015) proposed the following set of key indicators [20]:

- Material size of the processed materials (PMs): PMs (gigatons, Gt) and tons per capita (t/cap);
- Stock growth: Net addition to stocks as share of PMs (%);

[18] Haas, W., Krausmann, F., Wiedenhofer, D., & Heinz, M. (2015). How circular is the global economy?: An assessment of material flows, waste production, and recycling in the European Union and the world in 2005. *Journal of Industrial Ecology, 19*(5), 765-777.

[19] Eurostat. 2012. Economy-wide material flow accounts (EW-MFA). Compilation guide 2012. Luxembourg: Eurostat.

[20] Haas et al. (2015). *Ibidem*.

- Degree of circularity within the economy: Recycling as share of PMs (%);
- Biodegradable flows: Biomass as share of PMs (%);
- Throughput: DPO as share of PMs (%);
- Flows either biodegradable or recycled in economy as share of PM;
- Fossil energy carriers as share of PM;
- Material for energetic use as share of PM;
- Material for material use as share of PM;
- Waste rock as share of PM;
- Short-lived products as share of PM;
- EOL waste as share of PM;
- Recycling as share of EOL waste (overall recycling rate).

As Figure 2 shows, the recycling principle can be activated only when there is a circular economy system that supports its implementation. Such a system is composed of three steps, which create a continuous loop and ensure circularity:

- ***Step 1: Collection and Processing.*** Firms and governments must identify the best collection option for the involved society, choosing from among such options as curbside collection, drop-off centers, and deposits. The collection is followed by sustainable operations activities through which recyclables are sent to a specialized recovery facility to be sorted, cleaned, and processed into materials.
- ***Step 2: Manufacturing.*** Once the material is obtained, the collectors must identify the products and, more generally, the potential output that can be manufactured by using recycling materials. As previously mentioned, the EU Directives impose a certain percentage of recycling materials and recycled content. Collectors and authorities must then build a map of possible buyers for the recycled materials as a prerequisite to initiate any circular economy project. This need has led to stringent legislation and constraints, which have made recycling common to many applications like newspapers and paper towels, aluminium, plastic, and glass soft drink containers, steel cans, plastic laundry detergent bottles and more.
- ***Step 3: Purchasing New Products Made from Recycled Materials.*** Circular economy systems can require – considering the various markets – important changes in the current markets as well as the identification of new and emerging markets. Both options depend on both the economics and the marketing levers (which will be discussed in Chapter 2) that firms need to evaluate and activate to make circular economy systems sources of value rather than causes of business deterioration.

According to the Environmental Protection Agency (EPA), recycling content can be presented to the market in three forms, namely: *Recycled content product, recyclable product,* and *post-consumer content*[21]. The *recycled content product* are products made by using recycled materials that is either collected from an ad hoc recycling program or recovered from waste during traditional business processes like manufacturing and procurement. The firms are supposed to display on the label the percentage of recycled content to give full visibility and transparency to consumers. The *recyclable product* represents an important source for circular economy systems to accumulate the required feedstock. Those are products that can be collected, processed, and manufactured into new products after they have been used. Depending on the type of products, these items can be made either by virgin material only or by a certain percentage of recycled material. Therefore, the recycling activities and the value of returns highly depend on the product composition and the related level of recyclability. Finally, *post-consumer content* are the same types of items as recyclable content, with the main difference being the targets of the circular economy program. In fact, post-consumer content means items for which circular systems have a certain degree of interest and implies the adoption of specific take-back and recycling programs.

As explained by EP&C[22], recycling is defined as any recovery operation by which end-of-life waste is reprocessed into products, materials, or substances that can serve the original or comparable purposes. However, several details should be given regarding this definition with a particular lens on the difference between downcycling and upcycling.

Downcycling plays an important role that can be defined as the reprocessing of end-of-life (EOL) waste into products of inferior quality compared to the virgin material[23]. Therefore, downcycling implies a lower value and quality than the original product. There are sectors in which downcycling is heavily present, and it is even used as a synonym of recycling. The textile industry is one of those[24], and its flows and cycling opportunities are displayed in Figure 3.

---

[21] Environmental Protection Agency (EPA). https://www.epa.gov/recycle/recycling-basics.

[22] EP&C (European Parliament and Council). 2008. Waste directive 2008/98. http://europa.eu/legislation_summaries/environment/waste_management/ev0010_en.htm. Accessed November 2021.

[23] Haas et al. (2018). *Ibidem.*

[24] Sandin, G., & Peters, G.M. (2018). Environmental impact of textile reuse and recycling – A review. *Journal of Cleaner Production, 184*, 353-365.

Figure 3. Circular economy in the textile industry.

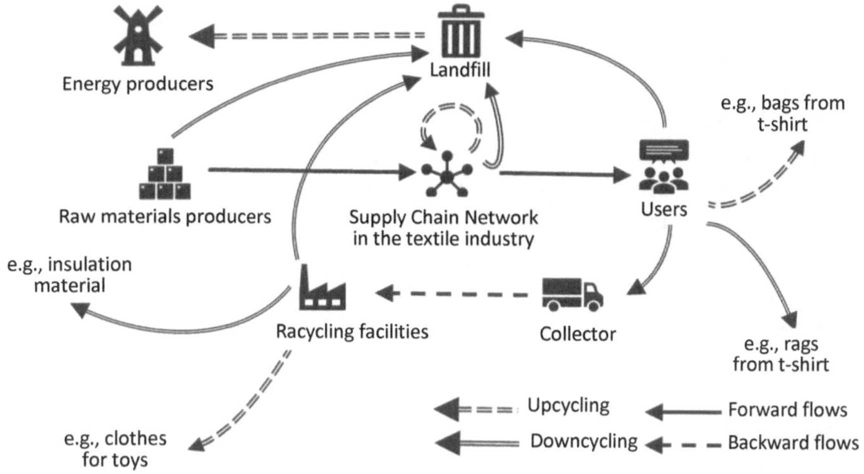

As shown in Figure 3, clothing and home textiles can be downcycled into other items, for example, industrial rags, low-grade blankets, insulation materials, and upholstery[25]. Because the length and the properties of the textile fibers, which form their structure, are reduced and altered by wear and laundry, the recycling process of either fabric or fiber yields materials of lower quality than materials made from virgin fibers. Thus, although fabric and fibers have a high capacity to be recycled, they are typically considered to be downcycled. In fact, the level of fiber quality obtained implies low final product quality, which can be measured in terms of aesthetics, fit-for-purpose, or material quality[26].

In contrast, polymer, oligomer, and monomer recycling typically yields fibers of similar quality to virgin fibers. Therefore, the recycling processes linked to such content yield upcycling. In general, upcycling is defined as a product from recycled material that is of higher or similar value and quality than the original product. According to Sung and Sung (2015), upcycling represents a set of practices and processes by means of which "old" products are modified and get a second life; hence, old content is turned into "new" content that has similar or more value than the original value[27]. In

[25] Schmidt, J.J., Gagnon, G.A., & Jamieson, R.C. (2016). Microalgae growth and phosphorus uptake in wastewater under simulated cold region conditions. *Ecological Engineering*, *95*, 588-593.

[26] Haas et al. (2018). *Ibidem*.

[27] Sung, K., & Sung, K. (2015, April). A review on upcycling: Current body of literature, knowledge gaps and a way forward. World Academy of Science, Engineering and Technology.

other frameworks, upcycling can also be applied to obtain materials or items that get to be re-adapted and/or re-purposed in a creative way, always with the same objective of expanding their lifespan. McDonough and Braungart[28] are the pioneers of upcycling and stress the importance of two factors linked to upcycling. First, upcycling should be included in the product design from the beginning to guarantee a high value of return through circular economy systems. Second, which is linked to the first factor, upcycling requires radical innovation, since the business routines and practices as well as the whole corporate strategy can undergo important changes and profound modifications.

Going back to Figure 3, the scope of products made by upcycling varies and ranges from rugs to fabric scraps to refashioned clothes. However, firms should be aware of the waste hierarchy when deciding which recycling approach to undertake. The fact that fiber and fabric recycling lead to downcycling and low fiber quality does not signify that they are less preferable to the upcycling of polymers, oligomers, or monomers. In fact, an analysis of the circular economy system should consider various factors when choosing a recycling framework. Factors may include the existing market for low quality textiles, the amount of energy and the environmental impact of both recycling approaches, and the social recognition linked to the recycling strategies. In general terms, firms need to include recycling decisions within their corporate strategy by using a cascade approach in which the textile waste first enters downcycling operations by reworking the fabric or fiber; once these have been damaged and downcycling is not an option any more, recycling operations can be activated by working on polymer, oligomer, or monomer recycling.

Indeed, the applications available for recycling are various and involve many industries and sectors. We refer the readers to surveys in sectors like metals and aluminum[29], paper[30], glass[31], battery[32], and plastic[33].

---

[28] McDonough, W., & Braungart, M. (2010). *Cradle to cradle: Remaking the way we make things*. North point press.

[29] Gaustad, G., Olivetti, E., & Kirchain, R. (2012). Improving aluminum recycling: A survey of sorting and impurity removal technologies. *Resources, Conservation and Recycling*, *58*, 79-87.

[30] Pivnenko, K., Olsson, M.E., Götze, R., Eriksson, E., & Astrup, T.F. (2016). Quantification of chemical contaminants in the paper and board fractions of municipal solid waste. *Waste Management*, *51*, 43-54.

[31] Lin, K.Y. (2018). User experience-based product design for smart production to empower industry 4.0 in the glass recycling circular economy. *Computers & Industrial Engineering*, *125*, 729-738.

[32] Velázquez-Martínez, O., Valio, J., Santasalo-Aarnio, A., Reuter, M., & Serna-

1.6. Alternative options to the circular economy

As displayed in Figure 1, the remaining principles of the waste cascade are prevention, energy recovery, and disposal. These principles are summarized here to complete the discussion on the waste pyramid and cascade, although there is a less strong connection with circular economy. In fact, these represent alternatives to circular economy systems that are, as described below, less beneficial in terms of triple bottom line.

The *prevention* principle assumes that materials and goods share one important point: They will become waste one day or another. Hence, the first target to be achieved is the creation of materials and goods that prevent waste from arising and accumulating. In fact, less waste leads to less need for reengineering the products for extended reuse, less disposal operations and, above all, less waste to be sent to landfills. Therefore, waste prevention requires important investments in R&D to design materials and goods that avoid unnecessary ingredients and reduce hazardous waste as much as possible. However, a very challenging trade off raises for firms in this scenario: Preventing the materials and goods from becoming waste also prevents the circular economy system from accumulating sufficient feedstock to justify its implementation.

The issues and challenges linked to waste reduction have been widely discussed by various governments and authorities. The European Commission[34], for example, estimates that European citizens generate around 5 tons of waste, of which only a limited share (39% for 2014 with a total EU waste production of 2.6 billion tons) is recycled and treated properly, while the rest still goes to either landfills or incinerators. However, when firms implement prevention strategies, confusion emerges when differentiating between "zero waste to landfill" and "zero waste". These terms have important differences, and confusing them can lead to greenwashing critics for the firms' brands.

"Zero waste" is a principle linked to the famous lead philosophy that has several overlaps with the principles of the waste hierarchy. Compa-

---

Guerrero, R. (2019). A critical review of lithium-ion battery recycling processes from a circular economy perspective. *Batteries*, *5*(4), 68.

[33] Gu, F., Guo, J., Zhang, W., Summers, P.A., & Hall, P. (2017). From waste plastics to industrial raw materials: A life cycle assessment of mechanical plastic recycling practice based on a real-world case study. *Science of the Total Environment*, *601*, 1192-1207.

[34] European Commission (2022). Waste Prevention and Management, https://ec.europa.eu/environment/green-growth/waste-prevention-and-management/index_en.htm (last accessed: January 2022).

nies frequently undertake zero-waste initiatives and incorporate them within their corporate strategy by reshaping long-term targets and market positioning[35]. For example, Whirlpool has initiated the #PlasticLess project to achieve zero waste to landfill by 2022. However, as reported by Axil (2022), the majority of businesses can only pursue zero waste targets when investing huge amounts of money in sustainability. In fact, that target may require a complete product redesign as well as radical changes in the supply chain management processes, business models, and infrastructure[36]. In contrast, "zero waste to landfill" is a specific and feasible target that almost any business can achieve. Rather than being obsessed with eliminating waste by modifying the whole business model along with each tier of the supply chain, zero waste to landfill practices aim at diverting existing waste away from landfills. This action can be put into practice in two ways: 1. implementing an ad hoc circular system that is pursued through reducing and reusing, and 2. by sending waste to energy recovery facilities.

Although it is a valid and feasible option, *energy recovery* represents one principle of the waste cascade that is far from being connected to circular economy systems. Non-recyclable waste can be diverted from landfills and sent to an energy for waste facility, which consists of a specialist plant converting waste into energy, most likely electricity. Indeed, the whole process does not come without adopting and managing sustainable operations. For example, the converting plant can carry out sorting activities by separating recyclable materials from the residual waste to be burnt to generate steam that is later converted into electricity. Similarly, the smoke resulting from the burning process can be very dangerous and requires sustainable operations based on smoke filtration to prevent contaminants from being released into the atmosphere. The type of sustainable operations that converting plants can pursue varies according to the country where it is located and the related regulations for different types of waste. For example, the environmental regulations allowing the leftover ash to be recycled into aggregate and other contents have been very well established in Europe by Directive 2010/75/EU[37], which also identifies the criteria according to which the residual ash can be dumped in landfills. Accordingly, the Directive establishes the operating conditions that ensure the proper conver-

[35] Axil (2022). How to achieve zero waste to landfill status. https://axil-is.com/how-to-achieve-zero-waste-landfill-status/(last accessed: January 2022).

[36] Axil (2022). *Ibidem*.

[37] Directive 2010/75/EU. https://eur-lex.europa.eu/legal-content/EN/TXT/?uri=celex%3A32010L0075.

sion of waste in such a manner that the resulting bottom ashes show either total organic carbon contents lower than 3 wt% or their loss on ignition is less than 5 wt% [38].

Although these restrictions are present, energy recovery represents a valid option to reduce waste and uses incinerating plants for all disposal operations. In fact, the combustion process allows one to reduce up to 90% of the volume of incoming waste and up to 70% of their solid mass, while making energy in the form of electricity and heat. From waste that does not exceed the carbonization process, it is possible to obtain large quantities of iron and non-ferrous materials (aluminium and copper) that are returned to the market. Other waste results in the waste of clean sand or granulated stones that are useful for concrete and asphalt. Finally, further material is recovered from the exhaust fumes, such as plaster and salt for defrosting. All these argumentation support the adoption of incinerators to avoid a large part of the costs related to sorting, evaluating, and managing the waste, which can also come from heterogeneous sources like biological, hygienic, and health-related waste: The high temperature of energy recovery plants destroys germs and harmful chemicals, thereby reducing contamination risks. Despite these various opportunities, energy recovery has many disadvantages, which can be summarized as follows: high capex, since the installation of an incineration plant is an expensive process and has high operating and maintenance costs; health risk for workers, who are often in contact with toxic materials and gases in the processing procedures; and pollutants, since the incineration does not eliminate the emission of dioxins in the exhaust fumes while making smoke that includes acid gases, carcinogenic dioxins, particulates, heavy metals, and nitrogen oxide. These gases are poisonous to the environment for the following motivations:

- The final ash production is highly toxic: Ash waste can potentially harm people and the environment. Although the ash that remains from the process may be relatively small in quantity, it contains several poisons and heavy metals that require further treatments. If not disposed of correctly, it can cause serious damage to the population and the environment.

[38] Blasenbauer, D., Huber, F., Lederer, J., Quina, M.J., Blanc-Biscarat, D., Bogush, A., Bontempi, E., Blondeau, J., Chimenos, J.M., Dahlbo, H., Fagerqvist, J., Giro-Paloma, J., Hjemmar, O., Hyks, J., Keaney, J., Lupsea-Toader, M., O'Caollai, C.J., Orupold, K., Pajak, T., Simon, F.G., Svecova, L., Syc, M., Ulvang, R., Vaajasaari, K., van Caneghem, J., van Zomeren, A., Vasarevicius, S., Wegner, K. & Fellner, J. (2020). Legal situation and current practice of waste incineration bottom ash utilisation in Europe. *Waste Management*, *102*, 868-883.

- Incinerators do not completely eliminate waste volume: Considering the high volumes that landfills occupy and the high costs associated and environmental impact resulting from the construction of incinerator plants, the plants are often unable to manage the amount of waste in the landfills.
- Logistics issues: These are associated with the distance from the waste location. Operating centers of cities and the gases released during transport could then impact the environment.
- Social disapproval because of air pollution: Generally, the public's perception of incinerators and landfills is one of disapproval, and they are perceived negatively. Current incineration models or general models are not widely supported by the general public, which has a perception that landfills and incinerators are negative to the environment, especially with the resulting emissions and risks for worker's health.

When the waste cannot be disposed of, it then goes to the landfill. Although the technologies to properly manage circular economy systems have progressed significantly in the last years, landfilling remains the most widespread and cheapest solution to treat and manage waste. Consequently, it also represents the major source of contamination and pollution. Developing countries have developed various landfill technologies to reduce the contamination level of the landfill by designing systems that minimize the impact on both the environment and human health. Although several projects have been highly successful, traditional landfills all over the world still face the problem of being abandoned without the implementation of proper safety features, implying a huge impact on the ecosystem.

Modern landfill facilities guarantee the hygienic treatment of waste, have low hazardous material entering the facility, have abandoned harmful burning practices, and protect both surface water and groundwater resources. In recent years, the adoption of a bottom line under the facilities has favored the achievement of more positive results. Further, emerging landfills are also required to guarantee waste pretreatment before the final disposal and, consequently, reduce the volume of waste, accelerate waste stabilization, and avoid eco-system contamination. In modern landfills, waste is frequently isolated from the groundwater through a base seal system, which is integrated within the whole landfill system, to prevent and/or control the intrusion of any type of precipitation into the waste. One feasible example is dry-tomb landfilling, which aims to avoid the incursion of water and, consequently, reduces the risks of gas and leachate. Alternatively, landfills can accommodate new bioreactor systems to solve the issues of waste storage and treatment, especially regarding organic content. The bioreactor allows the landfill to degrade the waste by using microorganisms and make, at the same time, biogas with high methane concentration, which can serve as a source of renewable energy. Finally, landfills managing the waste through nuclear technologies represent a future option to solve part of the remaining problems linked to waste disposal. Nuclear technologies are currently used dispose of marine plastic and manage the waste introduced by COVID-19, like masks, gloves, and other protective equipment[39].

[39] Trajano, J.C. (2021). Battling Marine Plastic Waste: Nuclear Technology's Role. RSIS Commentary, www.rsis.edu.sg.

Chapter 2

CIRCULAR NETWORKS AND ENGAGEMENT STRATEGIES

Pietro De Giovanni

ABSTRACT: *This chapter highlights the need for creating ad hoc networks of relationships when implementing circular economy systems. The network should be created according to both the consumers' and the collectors' needs to solve any logistics problems linked to circularity. The presence of strategic consumers can complicate identification of the proper circular network, requiring the adoption of the right return approach.*

2.1. Network creation in a circular economy

The implementation of a circular economy system requires the creation of a network in which firms, consumers, and collectors play a role. In fact, sustainable and responsible behavior towards the environment and society at large induce people and firms to make end-of-life/use goods available within the circular system. Genc and De Giovanni (2021) highlighted the role that issues like pollution, global warming, overpopulation, waste disposal, ocean acidification, deforestation, and ozone depletion have in society at large. Such issues cause society to become very preoccupied on the current and future state of the planet, creating new concerns and atypical emotions among individuals and groups [1]. This translates into stakeholders being conscious towards the impact of the circular economy and makes them recognize the importance of actions, projects, and practices aimed at building a circular economy.

The efforts of consumers, firms, and collectors in closing the loops originated by circular economy targets should converge in the optimization of an effective reverse logistics network through which feedstock can be properly collected and injected into the circular economy processes. The

[1] Genc, T.S., & De Giovanni, P. (2021). Dynamic pricing and green investments under conscious, emotional, and rational consumers. *Cleaner and Responsible Consumption*, 2, 100007.

creation of an ad hoc network represents, then, the key strategic ingredient to collect sufficient feedstock and make sure that sustainable operations can be activated after their collection. Figure 1 captures the idea of the types of relationships to be established with the circular economy network.

Figure 1. Circular Supply Chain.

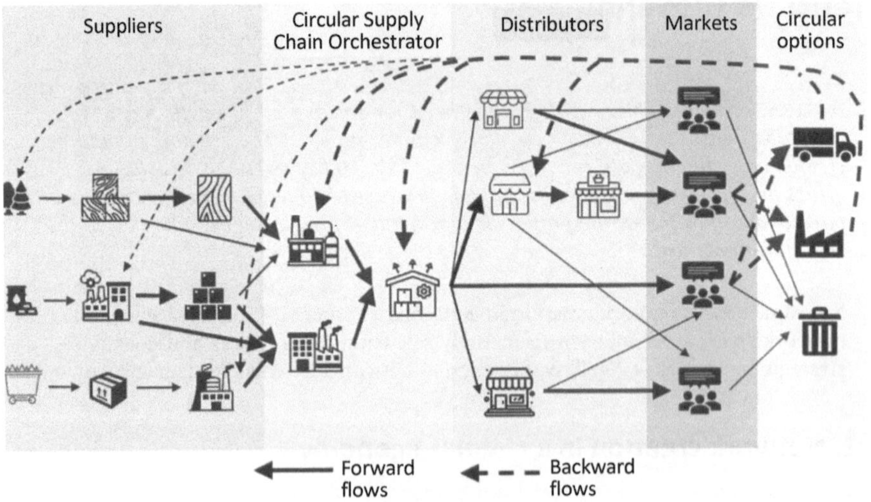

The first point that companies should have in mind is that the circular economy processes must be managed by integrating both the forward flows and reverse flows. The former originates from companies to the customers and allows the business models to be successful by reaching the market through proper outputs. Traditional operational levers, like quality and price, ensure business sustainability and include many other business aspects like service, stock availability, and warranty. Reverse flows connect the market to the companies, through which consumers return goods that have reached either the end-of-life stage or the end of use stage. In the first case, the products are not suitable for satisfying consumer's basic needs, while the natural reduction of the product's performance requires a repurchase to continue to satisfy those needs. In the second case, the goods are returned through the circular economy following customers' intentions to replace them, with several motivations, including the existence of a new release in the market or new legislation imposing a substitution. In both cases, the products are injected within the circular economy system and are treated differently according to the various blocks analyzed in the waste cascade.

The second point emerging from Figure 1 consists of the analysis of the various tiers existing in the closed loop supply chain. The tiers can be analyzed from both vertical and horizontal points of view. A vertical analysis reveals the number of firms within the same tier. Indeed, the higher the number of firms within one tier, the higher the chance to sell the products to customers and to collect them afterwards through reverse logistics activities. The horizontal dimension, instead, considers the number of tiers that compose the circular supply chain network. The higher the number of tiers, the more the closed loop supply chain is extended and, consequently, the management of both forward and backward flows becomes considerably complex. For example, a high number of tiers in the downstream of the chain signifies that the manufacturers have important difficulties in reaching the final customers and, at the same time, signals the complexity and difficulties in collecting content from customers in the future.

The last dimension to be analyzed is the presence of partners and strategic customers within the supply chain and circular economy networks. The bolded connections in the figure inform that two firms are strategic partners because they trust each other, they commit resources to close the loop of the circular economy, they have a certain degree of interdependency, and they have signed contracts and agreements lasting for long time periods. Should one of those firms exit the network, a big part of the overall business would disappear. The unbolded lines, instead, link firms and stakeholders through non-strategic connections, for which the circular economy is a sporadic business, the level of interdependency is very low, and other features like trust, organization compatibility, and leadership positions are simply less important. The success of a circular economy system is clear linked to the winning relationships established with the strategic suppliers and partners rather than with the others. Considering the overall set of relationships resulting from a certain network, the circular economy should also take into consideration some possible future relationships that can be established with new markets, new firms, new suppliers, as well as with atypical players like associations and 3PLs. In all these cases, companies are interested in pursuing some monitoring activities to evaluate future evolution of the corporate strategy and the related changes to the circular economy systems.

The presence of different types of flows, many tiers, and various types of relationships require that the circular economy is managed through an ad hoc circular supply chain orchestrator. This orchestrator coordinates across all supply chain processes, including circular economy activities. Typically, the orchestrator carries out optimization activities to integrate the key processes and procedures to reach high level of demand planning, efficiency, economic outcomes, sustainable targets, compliance with regulations, and to ensure that the overall system works with objectives inspired by ethics and human rights. Since the orchestrators' tasks are very broad, this position is filled by someone with enough power to influence all aspects of the supply chain, for example the brand owner of the entire business model, the technology innovators and owners of the intellectual property, or an influential logistician. Within all the possible activities that the orchestrator is asked to carry out, the engagement of both customers and collectors is one key point in the implementation of an ad hoc and successful network in circular economy.

2.2. Creating circular networks with consumer engagement

Consumer behaviors oriented to circularity are the starting points for the orchestrator to guarantee that any circular economy-based project can be pursued successfully. When consumers undertake unsustainable returning options, for example by landfilling goods that can be instead reused or recycled, the circular economy system does not have the right input or feedstock to activate and strategically justify the circular system. According to a survey by Islam et al. (2021), consumers' behavior and motivations to contribute to closing the loops within circular economy systems can depend on many factors[2]. Mature and modern consumers are aware of the negative damage that unsustainable behaviors have on the environment. However, some clusters of consumers do not have the sufficient knowledge to assess how harmful certain goods are for the ecosystem. This issue can be linked to a multitude of dimensions, like the lack of information on the goods' toxicity, lack of awareness, and insufficient information. Botelho et al. (2016) found that socio-demographic factors like age and gender can significantly affect consumers' motivation to return goods[3]. Furthermore, some consumers can perceive the whole returning system to be highly time consuming and complicated, making them unwilling to send back end-of-life/use products to the right circular facility[4]. Consumers can also be influenced by behavioral factors associated with the motivation to adopt en-

---

[2] Islam, M.T., Huda, N., Baumber, A., Shumon, R., Zaman, A., Ali, F., ... & Sahajwalla, V. (2021). A global review of consumer behavior towards e-waste and implications for the circular economy. *Journal of Cleaner Production*, *316*, 128297.

[3] Botelho, A., Ferreira Dias, M., Ferreira, C., & Pinto, L.M.C. (2016). The market of electrical and electronic equipment waste in Portugal: Analysis of take-back consumers' decisions. *Waste Management & Research*, *34*(10), 1074-1080.

[4] Gök, G., Tulun, Ş., & Gürbüz, O.A. (2017). Consumer Behavior and Policy About E-Waste in Aksaray and Niğde Cities, *Turkey. CLEAN-Soil, Air, Water*, *45*(7), 1500733.

vironment-friendly practices; specifically, moral norms, environmental beliefs, and social pressure can significantly affect the willingness to perform appropriate circular activities[5].

Considering the constellation of factors influencing consumers' willingness to return products and contribute to circularity, firms can either exploit the people's understanding of sustainable topics and their wish to preserve the environment and the planet for future generations, or they can identify ad hoc take-back programs to engage the community to return the products. In the former, the product return process and circular activities happen in a passive form, meaning that the return of products for reuse purposes depends on the people's voluntary actions. Therefore, it is called the *passive approach* to returns. However, public players like municipalities and governments have important roles in enhancing the people's willingness to adopt this behavior by investing in ad hoc facilities: People should be somehow facilitated to choose responsible behaviors by creating strategic networks of collecting points, writing agile and simplified return procedures, and investing in logistics and assets to enable the returns. This approach to returns is also called the *waste-stream approach*[6], to highlight that the people's voluntary return actions are followed by the negligible stakeholders' wishes to collect and take such returns. This feeling depends on the low value of returns, which can make the whole circular economy system not suitable from an economic perspective. However, other features discouraging stakeholders' targets for product collection can be linked to waste dimensions, toxicity, or the low impact on social factors. Finally, making used goods available for consumers can harm firms' sales, as consumers can find used products appealing and able to satisfy their needs while paying a much lower price than if they purchased those products new.

Together with the passive approach to returns, active return approaches can be undertaken to incentivize consumers in returning used products and, hence, activate the reuse principles. The *active return approach* presupposes the same assumptions of the passive return approach, that is, consumers are aware of the current environmental issues and have exerted a certain willingness to return products when those products reach their end-of-use stage. However, those consumers seek to receive an ad hoc incentive

---

[5] Siringo, R., Herdiansyah, H., & Kusumastuti, R.D. (2020). Underlying factors behind the low participation rate in electronic waste recycling. *Global Journal of Environmental Science and Management*, *6*(2), 203-214.

[6] Genc, T.S., & De Giovanni, P. (2017). Trade-in and save: A two-period closed-loop supply chain game with price and technology dependent returns. *International Journal of Production Economics*, *183*, 514-527.

for the contribution that they bring to the society and the environment. Therefore, consumers act in a strategic way knowing that there exists an immediate reward along with undertaking a certain behavior. This may represent a key lever for all myopic consumers, namely those people who perceive the environmental and global warming issues to be too far in the future to be their problem. Myopic consumers do not activate any return process unless an appealing incentive is given to them. The literature has presented several types of take-back programs through an active return approach within circular economy systems, which is also named the *value-stream approach*: Firms have a strong belief that a circular economy can be beneficial, especially in economic terms; therefore, efforts are put in place and programs are created to appropriate the returns' residual value and options for future repurchases. In modern economies and business models, take-back programs are part of firms' corporate strategies, since implying an immediate outflow of money should be counterbalanced by some benefits, such as a low amount of natural resources in the production processes, lower emissions, reputation, and trust. Examples of take-back programs to activate circular economy processes are:

- **Cash payments.** Customers who give back their old products are given cash for participating in the circular economy[7].
- **Tax discount.** Consumers returning products receive a rebate to be used to discount taxes in future years[8].
- **Discounts.** Firms guarantee a fixed discount percentage for new merchandise purchased with the use of cash/credit together with a product return[9].
- **Other advantages.** Customers who return their used products can obtain other types of advantages and incentives linked to different applications and sectors like tickets for cinemas and theaters, loyalty points, and options for advantages in services.

By using these take-back programs, the circular economy system can be analyzed in terms of capacity to collect used products through which an ac-

---

[7] Stewart, R., Niero, M., Murdock, K., & Olsen, S.I. (2018). Exploring the implementation of a circular economy strategy: The case of a closed-loop supply of aluminum beverage cans. *Procedia CIRP*, *69*, 810-815.

[8] Jalali, H., Ansaripoor, A., Ramani, V., & De Giovanni, P. (2021). Closed-loop supply chain models with coopetition options. *International Journal of Production Research*, 1-29.

[9] De Giovanni, P., & Zaccour, G. (2019). Optimal quality improvements and pricing strategies with active and passive product returns. *Omega*, *88*, 248-262.

tive return approach is guaranteed. Such capacity can then be measured by using the return function:

$$\textit{Return function} = \textit{Passive returns} + \textit{Active returns} + \textit{Stochastic returns}$$

in which the passive returns are directly linked to voluntary return approaches that consumers undertake, active returns derived from the incentives that activate the returning processes, and stochastic returns that come from unexpected sources of returns, like defective items or unattended deliveries. Indeed, the amplitude of the incentive determines the convenience of adopting a certain take-back program, which directly influences present and future purchasing and allows consumers to activate strategic behaviors.

2.3. Circular networks and consumers' strategic behaviors

Strategic behaviors refers to how consumers adjust their purchasing and returning intensions depending on some factors that can be either endogenous or exogenous to the product. The endogenous factors are the product features determining the incentives to be offered. Examples of these features include product quality, return residual value, warranty, or the maintenance operations pursued during the lifecycle; hence, high residual quality and value as well as valid warranty and correct maintenance lead to high incentives. There is a certain alignment between the incentives and firms' corporate strategy related to returns. Using the waste cascade helps considerably in determining the incentive: When the outcomes of the circular economy system are characterized by high levels of value, the incentive clearly increases proportionally; in contrast, when the same outcomes are suitable *only* for recycling operations, the incentive has a lower value.

Furthermore, the decision to return the products can also be linked to exogenous factors, that is, factors that are not dependent on the consumers. Rather, those factors are linked to decisions taken by all stakeholders surrounding the consumers. For example, governments can set environmental restrictions for the circulation of some classes of vehicles, thus forcing consumers to activate the return process and, then, inject inputs inside the circular economy system. The same may happen with other governmental instruments like taxes, bonuses, and incentives.

Firms' decisions also play an exogenous role in consumers' decisions. Investments in technology, R&D, and quality favor the activation of circular economy systems through the product replacement mechanism. Although goods did not reach the end-of-use stage of the lifecycle, the existence of a new version encourages consumers to return that product and get another in substitution. These situations enhance consumers' strategic behavior and, at the same time, the side effects for firms. The presence of consumers' strategic behavior can imply the creation of segments[10] as explained below:

- *Value exploiters:* Consumers who buy a high-tech product today and who continue to also use it also in the future even when a new version is released. These consumers do not activate any circular economy process although exogenous factors exist.
- *Earlier returners:* Consumers who buy a high-tech product today, use it for a certain amount of time, and replace it as soon as a new version is released by evaluating a rebate. The presence of an ad hoc trade-in program activates the circular economy through replacement mechanisms.
- *Rational returners:* Consumers who have no interest in purchasing today's release while they seek to purchase tomorrow's release, because their needs materialize only in a particular moment in time. These consumers do not take part in circular economy programs since they do not have input to form the feedstock.
- *Circular opportunists:* Consumers who renounce purchasing a high-tech product today to purchase it in the future at a discounted price while fully disregarding the latest releases. These consumers take advantage of the circular economy's outcomes to satisfy their needs.

The presence of these categories make firms aware that a circular economy system can lead to a complex market where consumers can be either rational, conscious, or emotional toward the circular economy[11]. Consumers are rational when they only think about their own utility function independent of the circular economy program. These consumers evaluate price, quality, R&D, and technology before diving into any contribution to circular economy systems. In contrast, emotional consumers do not take into consideration any of these features, since their sensitivity toward the environment and future generations makes them always look for the outcomes of circular economy systems, e.g., buying goods containing recycled material and being respectful of the environment. Finally, conscious consumers are sophisticated clusters and consider both the exogenous' firms features (e.g., price, quality) as well as the circular economy concerns (e.g., trade-in programs) when deciding how to treat and manage end-of-use/life goods.

---

[10] Liu, J., Zhai, X., & Chen, L. (2019). Optimal pricing strategy under trade-in program in the presence of strategic consumers. *Omega*, *84*, 1-17.

[11] Genc, T. and De Giovanni, P. (2021). *Ibidem*.

More in general, the presence of strategic consumers has an important economic impact on the feasibility of a circular economy system. It has been well-documented that consumers' strategic thinking can cause a delay of future purchasing, according to the idea that consumers anticipate future price decreases and postpone their purchases on purpose. Li et al. (2014) analyzed the presence of strategic consumers in the air travel industry [12], finding that 5.2% to 19.2% of the sampled population is strategic. Firms' product innovation and pricing strategies become considerably challenging as today's releases are highly suitable for current consumers as well as for future consumers. In fact, products are so over-designed and sophisticated that releases live in the marketplace even when a new generation of that product embeds the latest technologies and possesses unique and original features. When firms introduce new product releases, there is only a certain fraction of consumers who purchase the first product generation independent of the quality improvements and the price difference [13]. Yet, there exists another category of consumers that looks at the improvements as well as the price difference between releases before replacing a product [14]. Further, there is a certain segment of consumers that considers the quality/price offer not adequate and waits till the launch of a new release before purchasing the old product generation [15]. Finally, only a small category of consumers analyzes the circular economy outcomes and systems before deciding when to purchase [16].

The trade-in programs initiated within circular economy projects imply a premium, like a rebate or a bonus, that consumers receive if they replace their current product with a new release [17]. Therefore, rather than using rebates for traditional marketing targets (e.g., consumer retention and loyalty), circular economy systems can use rebates to mitigate the negative effect induced by strategic consumers' behavior. In a complex market characterized by the four segments earlier described, firms aiming at maximizing

[12] Li, J., Granados, N., & Netessine, S. (2014). Are consumers strategic? Structural estimation from the air-travel industry. *Management Science*, *60*(9), 2114-2137.

[13] Nair, H. (2007). Intertemporal price discrimination with forward-looking consumers: Application to the US market for console video-games. *Quantitative Marketing and Economics*, *5*(3), 239-292.

[14] De Giovanni, P. and Zaccour, G. (2019). *Ibidem.*

[15] Gowrisankaran, G., & Rysman, M. (2012). Dynamics of consumer demand for new durable goods. *Journal of Political Economy*, *120*(6), 1173-1219.

[16] Genc, T. and De Giovanni, P. (2021). *Ibidem.*

[17] Ray, S., Boyaci, T., & Aras, N. (2005). Optimal prices and trade-in rebates for durable, remanufacturable products. *Manufacturing & Service Operations Management*, *7*(3), 208-228.

their economic outcomes can set their price, discount, and rebate strategies to achieve their targets. Those segments interact each other and are characterized by heterogeneous willingness to pay for a certain product version as well as different quality perceptions and evaluations. On the one hand, the simultaneous presence of both discount programs and rebate programs makes firms even more exposed to consumers' strategic behavior. For example, some consumers might expect to receive an offer for a rebate before deciding whether to replace their goods. On the other hand, firms can play with more strategies to mitigate the negative effect induced by the presence of strategic consumers in the market and then optimize the overall flows linked to the circular economy system.

The use of trade-in programs should take into consideration the presence of strategic consumers and incentives to ensure the active return approach needed to make an overall evaluation of the various strategic clusters existing in the market. Beside the clusters that we mentioned earlier, several studies have shown the presence of strategic consumers within the context of the circular economy. When Original Equipment Manufacturers (OEM) sell durable goods, the market can consist of three strategic segments [18]: *Strategic consumers*, who purchase a product in the first period and decide whether to change it in the second period according to the residual quality; *cheapskates,* who always purchase used products; and *nonbuyers*, who systematically have nil utility from circular economy outcomes. Firms set a combination of price and trade in programs to optimize the profits in the presence of these segments.

The challenge that firms must solve is the integration of learning procedures and technologies within circular economy projects to identify the existence of strategic behaviors and set collecting policies, recycling facilities, and logistics networks. In fact, the presence of strategic consumers induces firms to select which blocks of the waste cascade to pursue as well as how to determine the business strategies. Hence, *how should firms set up a trade-in program to activate successful circular behaviors?* Several studies have pursued this direction. For example, Ray et al. (2005) combined pricing and trade-in rebate decisions for profit-maximizing manufacturers of durable goods [19]. Pricing schemes can be proposed in three versions: Uniform price for the entire market, age-independent price differentiation between new and replacement customers with constant rebates for replacement customers, and age-dependent price differentiation between new and replacement customers

---

[18] Chen, J.M., & Hsu, Y.T. (2015). Trade-ins strategy for a durable goods firm facing strategic consumers. *International Journal of Industrial Engineering*, 22(1), 183-194.

[19] Ray, S., Boyaci, T., & Aras, N. (2005). *Ibidem.*

with age-dependent rebates for replacement customers. Li et al. (2011) proposed trade-in programs in business-to-business markets where pricing and trade-in rebates co-exist to mitigate the negative effects of strategic consumers[20]. Those programs can look at rebates to anticipate their purchasing decisions according to the residual value of the first product generation and the expected incremental value of the second product generation. The benefits that trade-in programs supply can also be dynamic products are sold in two successive periods and delivered to two consumer generations[21]. Customers can take an active part in a trade-in program by paying a nonrefundable fee in the first period. Later, they can exercise the trade-in for a first-generation product by receiving a pre-specified trade-in value to be used when buying a second-generation product.

The studies that we reviewed above highlight how difficult it can be to close the loops of circular systems when consumers are heterogeneous. However, firms must solve these behavioral challenges, since the right trade-in programs can guarantee the proper accumulation of feedstock, which is the input for circular economy systems. The features that imply strategic behaviors allow consumers to first observe the latest products, for example, the quality of the products, the product's residual value, the warranty life, and the number of maintenance operations carried out over time, before deciding whether to trade in. This advantage that consumers have in making decisions according to private information is corroborated by the final voice that consumers have in the activation of circular economy processes; in fact, consumers evaluate the amplitude of a proposed incentive before returning their goods by analyzing the residual utility. Therefore, trade-in programs and the related incentives unlock the potential of circular economy systems.

2.4. Creating circular networks by collector engagement

As displayed in Figure 1, circular economy systems can require modifications to strategic thinking along with deep modifications to corporate strategy as well as important adjustments to all supply chain relationships. The main ingredient for implementing a successful circular economic system is to engage the companies responsible for the collection within the entire system. If the customer engagement is important to ensure the feedstock,

---

[20] Li, J., Granados, N., & Netessine, S. (2014). *Ibidem.*

[21] Yin, R., & Tang, C.S. (2014). Optimal temporal customer purchasing decisions under trade-in programs with up-front fees. *Decision Sciences*, *45*(3), 373-400.

then implementing a proper network of relationships allows the feedstock to be transported to the right facility, be treated and managed properly. The circular economy then becomes a logistic problem to be optimized by jointly considering the firms responsible for the forward process as well as the stakeholders who are responsible for the collection process. According to the supply chain theory, the involvement of multiple players and suppliers in the development of circular supply chain systems requires full involvement, commitments, joint investments, and the end pursuit of common goals and targets to increase the competitiveness of the whole network and the successfulness of the circular economy system. The importance of strong supply chain relationships management is well-documented in various research[22]. Such research has shown that 70% of the product cost refers to materials that are moved around the supply chain. Accordingly, supplier participation in green and circular economy initiatives foster the circular networks and ensure a mutual interdependency through which firms commit to common goals. Furthermore, the adoption of circular networks and strong supplier relationships lead to resources and knowledge sharing among all members, lower risks all over the chain, and an increase in the willingness to collaborate using long-term agreements.

According to this picture, the proper selection of stakeholders to be involved in the collection process is crucial for implementing a successful circular supply chain and, then, a circular network. Indeed, the criteria for selecting partners to close the loop go beyond the standard operational features like quantity, quality, and lead time and include green practices, programs, and attitudes. The new criteria for sustainable supplier selection can include environmental certifications, pollution control indicators, the level of substitution of discarded products with respect to original virgin materials, and processes implemented to make quality checks and disassembling operations greener[23]. The list of green criteria to be used for supplier selection have been widely studied in the literature and include eco-friendly materials and product design, green image, existence of an environmental management system, resource conservation and consumption, pollution control and prevention, training, level of service over the circular network, environmental certification, attitude in achieving sustainable development

[22] Duhaylongsod, J.B., & De Giovanni, P. (2018). The impact of innovation strategies on the relationship between supplier integration and operational performance. *International Journal of Physical Distribution & Logistics Management*. 49(2), 156-177.

[23] De Giovanni, P. (2020). An optimal control model with defective products and goodwill damages. *Annals of Operations Research*, *289*(2), 419-430.

goals, and also ethics, gender equality, and social norms[24].

Within the relational dimension, industrial symbiosis is progressively contributing to the development of circular economy systems. Industrial symbiosis refers to a network of firms that invest jointly in eco-solutions and integrate them by sharing their culture, goals, business, and expertise[25]. Therefore, the industrial symbiosis is a phenomenon much wider than a simple proximity strategy that focuses on physical resource exchanges. In fact, industrial symbiosis can involve all blocks of the waste cascade and then imply value opportunities toward circular economy systems. The industrial symbiosis should then be thought of as institutes to create and share knowledge among companies and to achieve two high-level targets, namely, industrial ecology and supply chain coordination.

Industrial ecology studies the stages of the production processes of goods and services from a point of view of nature, with the aim of mimicking the natural system by conserving and reusing the natural resources[26]. Industrial ecology can be seen as the scientific part of sustainability, as it studies the metabolism of industry[27], in which the industry is looked upon as an organism whose parts and components interact and integrate to resemble and mimic biological organisms for consuming, absorbing, and using any available source of material, input, and energy. Sullivan et al. (2018) mentioned three particular areas of management to be developed in modern business that link to industrial ecology[28]. First, there is a need to integrate the industrial ecology concept within the supply chain relationships by using a holistic approach to environmental management that also includes circular economy systems. Second, firms should gain expertise on the industrial ecology material flow studies, encouraging the management of scarce resources, energy, water, and materials while struggling to find effective waste management solutions. Third, industrial ecology requires supply chain members' willingness to modify commitments and strategic

---

[24] Gupta, S., Soni, U., & Kumar, G. (2019). Green supplier selection using multi-criterion decision making under fuzzy environment: A case study in automotive industry. *Computers & Industrial Engineering, 136*, 663-680.

[25] Maranesi, C., & De Giovanni, P. (2020). Modern circular economy: Corporate strategy, supply chain, and industrial symbiosis. *Sustainability, 12*(22), 9383.

[26] Chertow, M.R. (2008). Industrial ecology in a developing context. In *Sustainable development and environmental management* (pp. 335-349). Springer, Dordrecht.

[27] Jonker, G., & Harmsen, J. (2012). *Engineering for sustainability: a practical guide for sustainable design*. Elsevier.

[28] Sullivan, K., Thomas, S., & Rosano, M. (2018). Using industrial ecology and strategic management concepts to pursue the Sustainable Development Goals. *Journal of Cleaner Production, 174*, 237-246.

vision and incorporate new principles and culture[29]. Therefore, firms and supply chains still need to address the question of whether industrial ecology can complement and become part of strategic thinking and provide new opportunities for competitive advantage[30]. For example, within the business of wastewater management, several companies are now using industrial ecology principles to mimic the ecosystem of purifying wastewater using circular economy strategies. Instead of using traditional systems to purify water, manufacturers can partner with other firms in the energy sector using sustainable technologies to purify wastewater by capturing the CO_2 through microalgae; the latter plays the role of a "plant-like organism", since microalgae grow through photosynthesis with a combination of solar radiation, nutrients present in water, and the fluid's movement. While the purified water closes the circular loop by being injected in the manufacturer's plants for industrial purposes, the raised microalgae can be used for business opportunities in the industry of improving people's health, life, diet, and longevity.

While industrial ecology gives a voice to new forms of business opportunities and atypical circular economy systems, firms are challenged by identifying coordination mechanisms that also include circular economy aspects. De Giovanni and Zaccour (2022) defined coordination within closed loop systems as the identification of contracts and agreements through which firms form partnerships to simultaneously integrate both forward and backward flows[31]. Hence, the main question to be answered is how firms engaged in circular economy systems can identify the best coordination mechanisms to achieve their economic, environmental, and social targets. Accordingly, the coordination mechanisms can take the form of contracts, agreements, outcomes of negotiations, or deals, which were analyzed in their study using game theory approaches. The managerial takeaways from that survey are presented from strategic and managerial perspectives:

- *Predetermined per-return incentive.* This incentive mechanism presupposes that the collector receives a given amount for any unit returned within the circular economy system. This is a fixed amount known in advance by the collector. In general, the incentive is proportional to the

---

[29] Korhonen, J. (2005). Industrial ecology for sustainable development: Six controversies in theory building. *Environmental Values*, 83-112.

[30] Hoffman, A.J., Corbett, C.J., Joglekar, N., & Wells, P. (2014). Industrial ecology as a source of competitive advantage. *Journal of Industrial Ecology*, *18*(5), 597-602.

[31] De Giovanni, P., & Zaccour, G. (2022). A selective survey of game-theoretic models of closed-loop supply chains. *Annals of Operations Research*, 1-40.

number of units returned, to their weight, or to the nominal amounts of resources returned.

- *Per-return incentive set ex-post.* According to this mechanism, the incentive is a guarantee to the collector that is set according to some specific parameters, which is generally defined in a contract. The incentive can then be set according to the quality of the collected content, the quantity collected through circularity, the logistics collection network, the capacity to pre-treat the material, the return's residual value, the product lifecycle stage, the R&D and digital technology investments, the green practices adopted, and the social contributions, existing certifications, market developments for the collected content usage, attractivity for other forms of incentives (e.g., from the government), the capacity to influence the public opinion, and/or the value of the brand.
- *Buy-back contracts.* This particular form of a contract allows a seller (e.g., stores, retailers, dealers) to send back the unsold goods to the manufacturers by the end of the season. Therefore, this contract activates circular economy processes in an atypical way, since it is not linked to the end-of-use/life content. Rather, the parties agree on the repurchasing price guaranteed to the manufacturers who collect the unsold goods and which is defined according to some margins as well as some ad hoc features that ensure that goods are resalable.
- *Revenue sharing contracts.* These contracts have been introduced in the context of supply chain coordination to manage forward flows while working on the circularity of financial flows (revenues) rather than on the circularity of goods. They aim at mitigating the double marginalization effect by removing the marginalization at the wholesale price level while ensuring to wholesalers a share of revenues. This contract can be applied in a circular economy by ensuring a share of the revenues originated by selling the content of the circular system. The share can vary according to all features described in the incentives set *ex post.*
- *Joint circular programs.* Firms collaborate in creating circular economy systems. The total amount of required investments include both the opex and the capex. The outcomes and the benefits obtainable from the circular economy are then proportionally shared according to the contribution that each firm gave in the implementation of the overall system.
- *Licensing contracts.* This contract involves a manufacturer (license holder) and a seller (licensee) of collected content. The content collected through the circular economy can be protected (e.g., a valid patent exists) and, consequently, the parties negotiate the fee that the reseller should ensure to the license holder to finally close the loop.

- *Leasing contracts.* Product leasing is a service model in which a user pays for the access and the usage of a product during a certain period. Manufacturers typically maintain ownership of the product and are responsible for delivery, maintenance, and all take-back activities. Leasing allows the circular economy system to mitigate uncertainty on quantity, quality, and timing of returns.

The earlier mentioned mechanisms are aimed at circular economy coordination, which is defined hereby as: *Negotiating and defining a contract, an agreement, or a deal through the circular economy system adopts an active return approach and, consequently, guarantees to all parties involved in the network to be better off compared to the adoption of a passive return approach.*

The question that remains to be solved in reaching a proper circular economy coordination consists of the network structure to be selected and the firm that covers the leadership position. The former links to the type of circular economy relationships to be established within the whole systems. Figure 2 makes a comprehensive analysis of all networks presented in the literature on circular economy and closed loop systems. Instead, the leadership position refers to the company that decides the type of network structure to be used, the coordination mechanisms to be applied, as well as the strategies. Indeed, for any given network structure, the leadership position can considerably change the way the circular economy system is engineered and managed.

One important point to highlight in the earlier mentioned mechanisms is that economic motivations contribute to identify a certain incentive. Along with such motivations, there might also be non-economic motivations to implement circular systems that should be included in a coordination agreement. By managing the return flows, a circular economy properly ensures that both end-of-use and end-of-life goods are not disposed of, hence, ensuring the minimization of the negative environmental and social externalities. Furthermore, governments can also establish some specific collection constraints by charging fees when some environmental and social targets are not achieved. Since the circular economy requires the implementation of some atypical processes (e.g., collection, refurbish, inspection, etc.), the firms involved need to offer more jobs to the community and achieve high social benefits. Finally, managing the circular economy systems allow firms to avoid competitors collecting their products, acquiring both operational and economic value from the returns, and using those returns to gain a better position, especially in the second-hand market.

Figure 2. Closed-loop Supply Chain structures. (M-Manufacturer, R-Retailer, eR-eRetailer, C-Collector, eC-eCollector, D-Distribution center, S-Supplier, G-Goodwill).

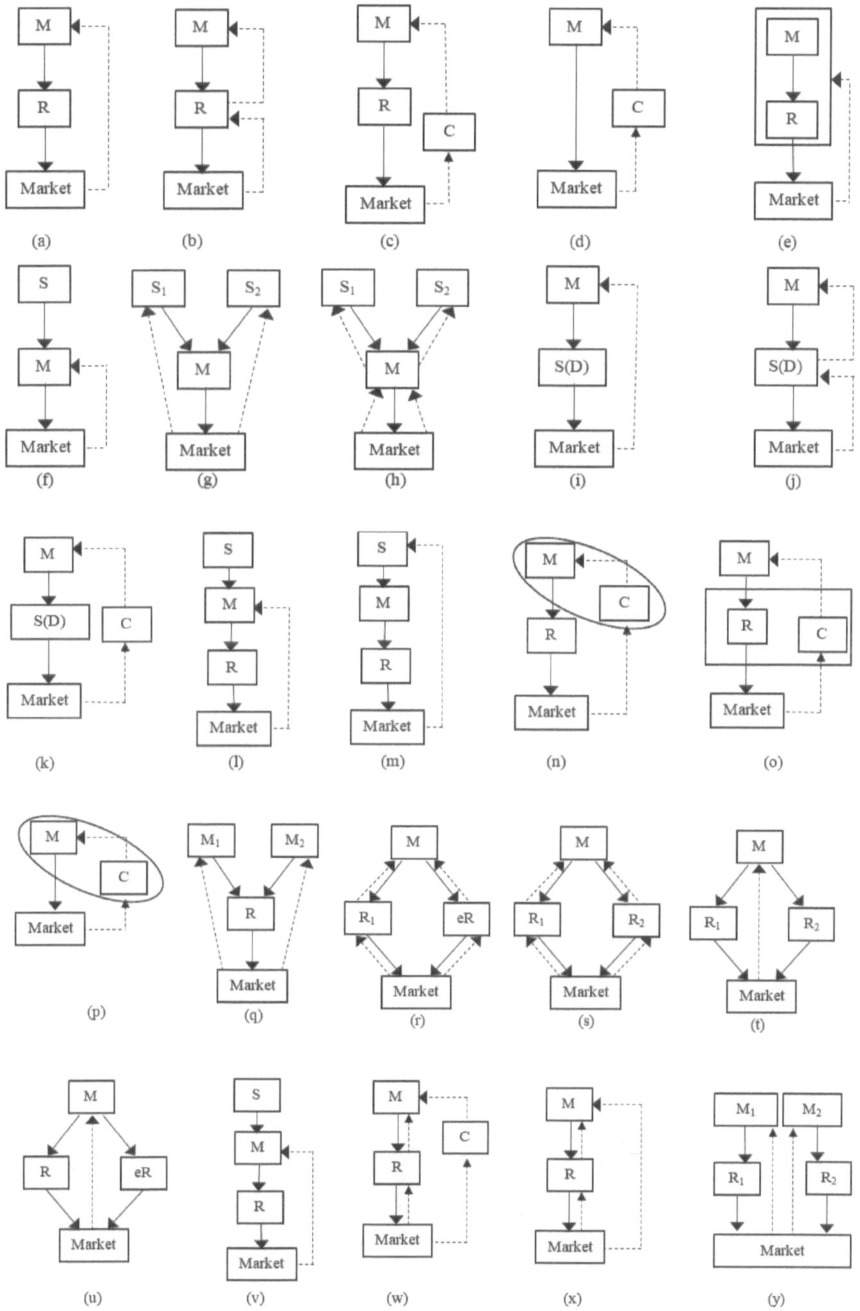

continued

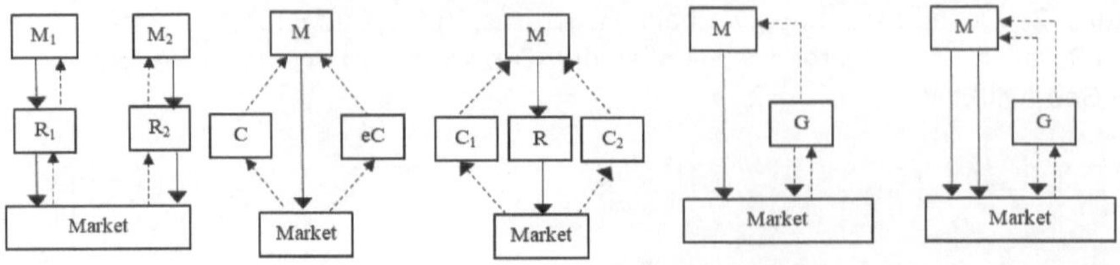
M1
M2
R1
R2
Market
M
C
eC
Market
M
C1
R
C2
Market
M
G
Market
M
G
Market

(z) (aa) (ab) (ac) (ad)

Chapter 3
CIRCULAR ECONOMY THROUGH PUBLIC INTERVENTIONS

Pietro De Giovanni

ABSTRACT: *This chapter screens the public incentive and the bonus schemes available for firms to initiate circular economy projects. Depending on the scheme, firms can access certain types of incentives and evaluate possible outcomes and benefits. Public interventions are vital in all cases in which the circular economy's content value is low, discouraging circular projects from being initiated.*

3.1. Review of public incentives to support circular economy systems

The public interventions to support circular economy projects function as real incentive mechanisms to scale-up investments in given countries and territories. In order for an incentive to be well-designed, it should create benefits for society at large and favor eco-system conditions to close the loops. Therefore, the purposes of incentives can be heterogeneous and of various types, aimed at supporting the commercial development of businesses linked to the circular economy, removing entry barriers to specific sectors or markets, favoring the adoption of new technology, developing original competences and skills, or injecting new capital to contribute to both capital expenditures (capex) and operating expenditures (opex).

Public schemes and interventions support circular economy systems that are already in place, as well as completely new circular-based projects. Under the former, the options available can be constrained by current circular economy policies and approaches, requiring the consultation of experts to evaluate which scheme may fit within the specific situation. In Italy, CONAI (Consorzio Nazionale Imballaggi [1] – the Italian consortium for packaging) offers expertise in providing solutions and options for firms aimed at improving their packaging from an environmental and social perspective. The consortium identifies proper schemes and paths to access public plans and programs, considering the current packaging structure and environmental impact. Under the latter, the circular economy system can be created ad hoc, also pursuing modern versions such as the smart circular economy (see Chapter 5).

In the remaining portion of the chapter, public incentives related to waste management and recycling activities are presented, through which firms can speed up the transition toward a more circular economy system. Such incentives can be either bonus incentives, which create opportunities for stakeholders, or malus incentives, which force stakeholders to modify their behavior. According to Couder et al. (2021), "*incentives aim at addressing market failures that prevent or delay the transition towards circular products, services and solutions. They play an instrumental role in pricing negative externalities, steering markets towards sustainability and driving behavioral changes. In addition, awareness-raising can be a powerful tool to complement incentives by empowering consumers to make more sustainable choices which, in return, may stimulate the market to offer more sustainable products and services at affordable prices* [2]*. Incentives have the ability to create value, de-risk investments and improve the competitiveness of value chains that bring net environmental benefits when compared with linear economies. They also yield benefits to the economy and society*". Table 1 summarizes the incentives and mechanisms made available by public authorities and distinguishes them in terms of malus and bonus incentives, stakeholders involved, relationship to the circular economy, connections to the waste pyramid and cascade, and associated business challenges.

---

[1] https://www.conai.org/en/.

[2] Couder, N., Katrakis, E., & Nacci, G. (2021). Incentive to boost the Circular Economy. A guide for Public Authorities. EU, Research and Innovation.

3.2. End-of-waste mechanism

The "end-of-waste" mechanism seeks to facilitate the adoption of procedures to sustainably treat waste and obtain mutual recognition of the possible outcomes. Since the end of waste is an industry-specific output, legislation and schemes are available for ad-hoc material treatments. Indeed, the uncertainty surrounding both the waste or product status of secondary raw materials raises important barriers to the development of effective policies and effectively guarantees the effectiveness of circular economy systems. In general, end-of-waste schemes favor the circulation of raw materials conditioned to meeting quality and industry standards allowing for the use of content as feedstock for sustainable operations. End-of-waste schemes can be implemented with an emphasis on efficiency, specifically by analyzing the possible economies of scales linked to some operations such as recycling. When certain waste ceases to be waste and becomes either a product or a secondary raw material, the circular economy system must demonstrate that its use will not lead to adverse environmental or human health impacts.

One major issue that must be solved in end-of-waste schemes is investment in transportation and logistics facilities. When the waste is moved within a certain territory or is even shipped in other countries, the content is somehow uncertain. This uncertainty does not allow the circular economy system to pursue its targets of closing the loops and rendering the waste circular. In contrast, available schemes should eventually be supported by other legislation facilitating the cross-border movement of waste materials, putting into actions stringent procedures to check the waste content and hence reduce the amount of administrative burdens supporting the scheme. End-of-waste incentives are fruitful when the output of the waste treatment can be easily sold in other markets or used in other industrial applications: These options increase overall recycling rates, reduce the amount of necessary resources, and valorize biomass waste and residues, such as bio-based materials or chemical feedstock.

3.3. Make standards more circular

Public incentives examining the standardization of materials and goods seek to favor the use of recycled materials, product reparability, reusability, and recyclability. Therefore, they play an important role in determining the standards to be applied in a certain industry, especially when it comes to the use of secondary material. In fact, the performance of secondary material must follow the same targets of the virgin material.

Firms accessing these incentives generally substitute virgin materials with secondary raw materials and adapt existing standards to guarantee high performance of the final good. Therefore, this incentive leads to a general increase in recyclable and reusable material and opens new market opportunities. At the same time, it can have important implications for the competition, which will be played out at another level, expressed in terms of green materials, selling price, and quality assurance.

3.4. Ban products when more circular alternatives exist

These interventions seek to push firms to adapt more circular solutions in terms of reducing the volume and the weight of packaging, favor the use of recycled goods or goods with high recycled content, and search for compostable materials that will add nutrients to the eco-system.

Firms must evaluate whether the traditional business strategies (e.g., pricing and advertising) are sufficient to discourage consumers from purchasing non-circular goods, while a general analysis of the social sphere is needed to understand the overall impact of banned goods. The proper design of circular goods is the secret to implementing a successful incentive by pursuing efficiency, durability, ease of disassembly, and repair (see Chapter 4 for more details on circular design).

From a market point of view, only a significant difference between circular and non-circular goods can justify a ban. Governments should introduce stringent controls to verify the products and the materials to be eventually substituted (e.g., presence of non-hazardous waste), especially for intercontinental purchases. The analysis of the circular materials and goods must be justified through a comprehensive review. The consensus is that the circular alternatives can be more expensive at the beginning of the life cycle.

3.5. Promote the social economy through activities fostering the circular economy

These incentives seek to promote social involvement in the collection, sorting, and repair of some specific waste streams (textiles, furniture). This incentive can have a radical impact on the social sphere, since new repair and reuse shops can be opened. Used products that are repaired and functionally and technically approved can be sold in the secondhand-market, targeted to low-income clusters of the population who normally cannot afford to buy such products, or sent to developing countries.

Incentives should be used for training purposes, as social workers need to carry out collecting, sorting, and repairing operations, requiring ad-hoc skills and competencies. Therefore, environmental development is followed by intense social development. Furthermore, all new shops and jobs can receive other types of incentives, such as low taxation rates and additional financial support.

3.6. Increase the guarantee period

The mechanism by which firms increase the warranty period is linked to the indirect need to increase product durability, which leads to longer life cycles. Although the product life cycle is extended, firms can still reduce it by launching new product releases or versions. In any case, consumers are responsible for proofing the guarantee period, which generally lasts two years.

Fewer products due to longer lifetimes thereby reduce the amount of waste produced over time and allow firms to use assets that would otherwise be discarded. Indeed, making goods more durable contrasts with the use of recycling material that does not align with quality standards. Durability can cause products to become heavier, using more materials and additives when it comes to treating them for circularity. This might generate increases in operating costs. At the same time, the opportunity to reuse and repair goods can promote new jobs and enhance the social economy.

3.7. Favor R&D support for integrated value-chain projects and investment in new circular activities

This incentive mechanism seeks to promote initiatives along the supply chain, with the purposes of integrating firms' business models, favoring joint investments, and seeking to establish well-functioning circular economy systems. Governments pay a fraction of the required investments, independent of the value chain tier subject to the intervention, and under the condition of highlighting the real contributions offered by the new circular economy project. Therefore, this mechanism can be fruitfully used in all circular supply chain frameworks in which collaboration among firms and stakeholders is absent while their integration can lead to improved circumstances. Due to its nature, this mechanism can be easily applied to all collaborative projects requiring considerable investments, such as, for example, the adoption of new technology requiring radical changes in the circular system.

3.8. Set up green deals and clusters at different levels

This kind of incentive can be effectively applied in all contexts in which the value chains are split into numerous, independent, and worldwide dispersed actors whose activities are not integrated, and whose related knowledge is very limited. While the traditional commercial relationships within global supply chains limit information sharing and exchange, this incentive mechanism can favor collaboration supporting the creation of clusters of firms that cover the supply chain stages and tiers, either globally or locally, and giving rise to new strategic paradigms such as industrial symbiosis and industrial ecology. These clusters can perform specific activities such as, for example, the creation of a laboratory and a research center to achieve ad-hoc green deals. Public authorities support these kinds of clusters through communication, legal help, and alignment with social and environmental targets. At the same time, with knowledge of the administrative machines of some public institutes, the incentive can require a long time to be implemented, rendering the green deals obsolete.

3.9. Favor environmental labeling and certification

One main challenge that circular economy systems face is to communicate with society at large about the real instruments and the true benefits obtained through circular actions and practices. Incentives based on favoring environmental labeling and certification seek to encourage consumers to engage in sustainable behaviors and choices by demonstrating the circular economy and sustainable impacts. Therefore, it seeks to truthfully demonstrate firms' commitments and wishes to preserve the environment through circular economy systems. This target is achieved by using environmental-based methodologies, employing public data, framing standard modeling, values and weighting factors and, above all else, computing the environmental impacts through standard, well-known methods.

Accordingly, on/off or semi-quantitative labels can be replaced by meaningful quantitative labels to enhance people's understanding of products within the same category from an environmental perspective as well as a social perspective. This mechanism increases competition among firms and, indeed, among circular economy systems, stimulating the achievement of social and environmental targets as a source of competitive advantage. Such incentives make firms aware of the need for investments and green commitments, stimulating innovation and research in circular economy practices while informing consumers through labels that have a positive impact on brand reputation and reliability.

3.10. Communication about the repair of products

Public authorities perceive that the incentives for designing products through circular principles are not very effective if consumers are not fully knowledgeable of the potential offered by circular economy content. Particular attention has been given to communication on repairing products, which seeks to extend the product's life cycle by informing consumers of their properties that are easily repaired. Clearly, this type of incentive seeks to modify consumers' habits and behaviors to contribute to circular economy targets by acquiring new and atypical skills such as sorting and reusing. Firms can provide ad-hoc dictionaries and digital content to favor the reparation of goods.

Indeed, the incentives cause some business externalities that should be matched with environmental and the social outcomes. Allowing consumers to repair their goods prevents them from repurchasing and replacing those goods, leading to a direct reduction of sales. This implies that firms can transfer a part of their lower future sales to consumers through higher prices. Furthermore, communication must be very effective since consumers have shown a lack of participation in such initiatives and an unwillingness to acquire new skills aimed at reparation. To avoid market distortions, public authorities can support product reparation by providing further subsidies and tax breaks.

3.11. Material taxation

This mechanism aims at capturing negative externalities that are generally visible from traditional economic levers such as prices, gas emissions, or eco-system degradation. To consider these externalities, public authorities can use material taxation, which is a de facto penalty mechanism aimed at incentivizing the use of green material. Among these mechanisms, public authorities have introduced tax mechanisms based on carbon, energy, resources, and material. Furthermore, positive incentives have taken the form of subsidies, whose amount is determined by evaluating public investment projects based on their full societal impact. The general idea behind these mechanisms is to reduce the amount of non-green material and natural resources used while making the business models more profitable.

Because the use of primary materials generates greater environmental impacts than the use of recycled materials, public authorities may decide to increase the relative price of primary materials compared to recycled materials. Clearly, to avoid market distortions, the price difference between virgin and recycled materials must be sufficiently high to cover the sustainable operations behind material reduction, reuse, and recycling, such as the cost of selective collection, sorting and recycling operations. In these instances, secondary materials become permanently competitive, and the circular economy is successful.

Since the supply chains are dispersed worldwide, public authorities can impose taxing impacts where they happen (e.g., emission or waste generation points), while related costs can be spread and integrated over the value chain. This implies that supply chain members can perceive pressures related to negative environmental impacts over the supply chain, even if they are not directly responsible for such externalities. In this way, all parties and stakeholders have an incentive to implement circular systems. The penalties associated with these mechanisms can either be fixed or variable. Under the former, they are associated with the unit of waste or emissions. Under the latter, they are associated with constraints and boundaries (e.g., emission trading schemes). Indeed, these schemes suffer from international trades and exchanges since they can vary from one country to another.

3.12. Modulation of EPR fees

The extended producer responsibility (EPR) is an environmental instrument public authorities can put into place to make producers responsible for managing the whole product's life cycle. For example, producers pay EPR fees based on quantities of products (e.g., electric and electronic equipment and textiles) placed in the market. The producers can pay such fees to ad-hoc institutions named producer responsibility organizations (PRO) in the case of a collective fulfilment of ERP.

The incentive elaborated by a public authority requires "modulation" since the fee can be computed according to different criteria, specifically:

- *A fee scale reflecting the real net cost of waste management.* Penalties can reflect the form of a malus for all circular systems not reaching certain targets (e.g., recycling targets) or a bonus when targets are achieved. Clearly, the magnitude of the scale is difficult to determine when goods have a long life cycle.
- *A fee scale with environmental bonus/malus to reflect differences in a product's environmental footprints within the fee scale.* The determination of the environmental differences between goods and circular goods challenges this incentive. The impacts are difficult to estimate and compare since they follow different life cycles.
- *A fee scale with bonus/malus established based on the expected impact on product design rather than on economic or environmental impacts.* In-

deed, this mechanism aims at favoring the circular design. However, the fee can create important externalities when consumers pay the cost for lack of product design.

- *A fee scale reflecting the full societal impact.* Circular systems must provide clear evidence of social impact before diving into such a mechanism. Therefore, the modulation can be challenging due to the absence of benchmarks.

Since the incentives are modulated according to the product design, the fees paid by producers are based on the goods' reparability, recyclability and/or recycled content. Hence, important differences among sectors may exist. Furthermore, the PRO can either be for profit or not-for-profit, giving rise to atypical forms of competition.

3.13. EPR: Adapting contract duration and conditions

Circular economy systems, especially when managed through passive return approaches (see Chapter 2), are very uncertain in terms of time, quantity, and quality of returns. Therefore, when EPR schemes are in place, contractors may exhibit some reluctance in making important investments in infrastructure and capex if the circular system does not ensure a sufficient amount of waste materials. Accordingly, public authorities have defined a mechanism to adopt the contract duration and conditions according to circular economy dynamics, which are most likely linked to reductions in economic and financial risks in their investments. All involved stakeholders can display a certain willingness to embrace this scheme to feel safer regarding the roles and responsibilities of all players involved in the circular system and absorb externalities not controllable within the contracts. For example, a decrease in price for the primary material leads to a lowering in the price of recycling materials, decreasing the overall economic convenience of the contractors' infrastructure.

A prerequisite for secure long-term investments is a robust and stable legislative framework. In countries in which the legislation and regulations change often, long-term investments are not viable unless adaptive contract duration and conditions can apply. Nonetheless, high capex may create important barriers for newcomers while favoring the creation of dangerous monopolistic frameworks.

3.14. Green public procurement: Apply environmental (circularity) criteria (global environmental performance, recycled content, long life)

This mechanism is linked to procurement activities for public expenditures, which should support the circularity of products and services. Indeed, the criteria to access for such a scheme link to the inclusion of environmental/circularity criteria in the purchasing process and apply environmental labels that demonstrate the use of circularity criteria in purchasing. Examples of circular practices to be undertaken when aiming at this incentive scheme are as follows: The reduction of over-packaging, longer product lifecycles, the availability of spare parts and related information for consumers, and the level of recyclability through identification of the amount of recycled content.

The role of public authorities in undertaking circular purchasing is fundamental in signaling the importance of this practice. When public authorities look for circular purchasing, producers must adjust their practices and align their targets to also become circular; otherwise, a big piece of the market linked to the public domain can be lost. Public authorities will be willing to pay higher prices for circular goods in the belief that sustainable products are more expensive than traditional goods. This has the effect of creating a new mindset in society according to which sustainable goods contribute to environmental protection and preservation and help new generations to achieve growth in a better environment. Hence, public authorities favor the departure from a myopic and short-term view linked to economic factors and embrace environmental and social outcomes. Furthermore, such willingness encourages producers to invest in eco-innovation and pursue more circular economy projects in the future.

3.15. Mandatory recycled content

A scheme that imposes a mandatory recycled content is most likely seen as a malus mechanism for firms that have old industrial systems, and constraints of this kind generally require radical system changes. Surely, this mechanism stimulates the demand for recycled materials and consequently favors access to other types of incentives supporting R&D investments and production facility upgrades. From an operational perspective, increasing the recycling scale allows recycling facilities and operators to increase recycling efficiency and, as a result, guarantee high accessibility to recycling materials from an economic point of view.

The mechanism can create some distortions since not all countries may apply it, and even in the case of application, the percentage of recycled content can differ substantially. Therefore, legislation should properly regulate the competition between domestic and foreign goods when this scheme is in place. Indeed, compulsory content is feasible for application when firms can access the outcomes of the circular economy, which can also differ when moving from one sector to another. Furthermore, there is a need for verification systems and algorithms since the recycling material can be compromised, especially in the presence of goods containing different types of materials, all of which can be introduced by either primary or secondary materials.

3.16. Landfill and incineration ban/tax

The current state of technology in landfills and incinerators does not guarantee circularity. Since technological changes require important investments, public authorities have identified some malus incentives every time firms send waste to landfills or incinerators with the objective of reducing this flow. Therefore, a ban and a tax, either singly or together, can be charged to firms preferring landfilling to circularity, which is proportional to both the type and the amount of waste. The fee is not quantified as it depends on various parameters, such as whether the waste has been sorted by containing recyclable and reusable materials. Typically, landfill taxes should be higher than incineration taxes, as incineration, which generates energy from waste, is somehow preferable to landfilling. Overall, sorting operations determine the fees applied to producers. Indeed, when waste materials come from households, the application of this mechanism is much more challenging due to the difficulties in associating the waste to its responsible source. From a social point of view, increasing bans and taxes for waste going to landfills and incinerators creates better feelings among members of society, who always look at these solutions as harmful and highly risky to their health.

3.17. Waste producers pay the full waste management cost

This scheme is highly diffused and applies to both households and firms. Defined as pay-as-you-throw, trash metering, or user pay, the mechanism is based on a rate that waste producers pay based on the amount of waste they present to the municipality or the local authority to be collected and treated. In some instances, the fee can be modelled according to other features, such as producer size and income. The scheme favors the adoption of circular solutions, which lead to recycling waste rather than residual waste. Furthermore, it compels waste producers to adopt responsible behaviors by changing their purchasing, consumption, and returning patterns, with the idea of avoiding disposal costs.

When analyzing the constellation of stakeholders contributing to circular systems, it clearly indicates that waste management cost seeks to impose financial burdens on everyone, including taxpayers, waste producers, suppliers, and consumers. Therefore, the mechanism encourages the entire value chain to undertake eco-design principles, reduce landfilling, and develop both recycling and recovery channels.

3.18. Lower VAT on green products and services

The mechanism linked to a lower tax for circular and sustainable goods rather than traditional products and services is very intuitive and appealing. However, it might be difficult to apply since the definition of circular goods is not unique. The criteria used to define a good as circular can depend on the life cycle, the returns' residual value, the level of recyclability, the percentage of recycled content, and emissions over the entire life cycle. Furthermore, the presence of an extended value chain can create other difficulties, as it becomes cumbersome to identify the place and the actor to apply the tax discount.

3.19. Addressing waste exports from the EU

Waste exports are among the most difficult processes to be monitored by the public authority since the waste can be contaminated and dangerous. Therefore, independent of how the fees can be computed, better enforcement of existing requirements and monitoring activities over the territory are essential to combat illegal exports of waste. Along with such penalties, public authorities must identify incentives for engaging in recycling and circular procedures and substitute hazardous materials with friendly materials. This requires investments in circular design, for which incentives are available. One possible explanation for public authorities engaging in the illegal export of waste is the marginal economic convenience behind selling secondary materials. Therefore, fees on illegal transport should be followed by measures to sponsor the secondary market by subsidizing the price of such materials, designating a certain percentage of recycling materials into goods, and sponsoring eco-design. Indeed, there is a certain relationship between the sources of waste and the effectiveness of this initiative. When there are numerous sources of waste, this implies that the waste materials have low economic value. As a result, imposing fees on waste transport can be ineffective due to the high amount of waste; rather, public authorities must intervene with policies aimed at properly reusing and recycling waste.

3.20. Tradable recycling credits schemes

This mechanism is very similar to the emission trading scheme. In fact, this is a tradable allowance system permitting the use of a certain amount of primary material on presentation of evidence that a certain amount of secondary material has been used "somewhere else". Adopting circular economy principles and using a large quantity of secondary materials generate a certain number of credits; all credits exceeding the minimum requirement can be sold to the end users of primary material to compensate for their unsustainable behaviors.

A tradable recycling credit mechanism generally acts on both the supply side and the demand side of a value chain, hence incentivizing circular value chains at large. Those credits can be generated for companies turning waste into secondary raw materials as a substitution for primary raw materials. Firms obligated to comply with certain recycled-content targets are also subject to this incentive option.

3.21. Subsidies

The subsidies provided by public authorities are financial rewards transferred from the public budget to private actors and stakeholders, which are engaged in adopting circular economy-based behaviors. The subsidies mechanism targets circular economy projects aimed at preventing market failures. In fact, the economic value obtained from the circular economy can be very negligible, rendering the entire framework economically unfeasible and unattractive (see Chapter 4). This reward ensures real monetary income, which covers either partially or totally the investments required for stakeholders to adjust their behaviors toward circularity.

The subsidy can take either the simple form of a direct transfer of money from a public agency to a private economic actor or can be designed according to the sought-after change in behaviors. Furthermore, it can be delivered in either a lump-sum payment or a variable and continuous set of payments that are dependent upon the targets achieved and the behavioral changes. The role of subsidies has been largely investigated in the circular economy and closed-loop supply chain framework to unlock the value of circularity and act for both capex and opex[3]. Moreover, subsidies can be used to develop circular economy industrial hubs, industrial symbiosis, large-scale installations, and services related to circularity. Since they link to public money spending, such subsidies can easily create distortions in the market; hence, they might be prohibited for motivations diverging from the circular economy and sustainability, as well as social and public outcomes, while retaining the features of being non-discriminatory, proportional to the circular economy project's targets, and short-term orientated relative to outgoing flows.

[3] De Giovanni, P., & Zaccour, G. (2022). A selective survey of game-theoretic models of closed-loop supply chains. *Annals of Operations Research*, 1-40.

Table 1. Public interventions to support circular economy.

Incentive	Bonus/Malus	Stakeholders involved	Link to circular economy	Connection to the waste cascade	Business opportunities	Business challenges
End-of-waste	Bonus	Manufacturers, retailers, stores, suppliers, collectors, landfills	Reduction and valorization of waste	Low value content in the end-of-life stage	Possible economies of scales and efficiency, remove cross-border constraints and facilitate the waste mobility	Quality to be checked and verified, industrial standards to be met, check for adverse environmental and human impact, transportation and logistics facilities, identification of a markets and alternative industrial applications
Make standards more circular	Bonus	Manufacturers, retailers, stores, suppliers	Use of recycled materials, product reparability, reusability, and recyclability	Medium value content in the end-of-life stage	New market opportunities through recyclable and reusable materials.	Secondary material should have the same standards of virgin material, guarantee high performance for the final product, new possible competitive threats.
Ban products when more circular alternatives exist	Malus	Manufacturers, retailers, stores, suppliers	Product design and substitution of non-circular material	High value content in the early lifecycle stage	Reducing the volume and the weight of packaging, favor the use of recycled goods or goods with high recycled content, and search for compostable materials that will add nutrients to the eco-system.	Find the business drivers to discourage consumer purchasing no-circular goods (e.g., price), investments in design, banning products can lead to social issues (e.g., people cannot afford circular goods), stringent controls for imported materials and goods

Promote the social economy through activities fostering the circular economy	Bonus	Collectors, retailers, stores, people	Waste collection, reparation, and reuse	Medium value content in the end-of-life stage	Opening of new shops and business opportunities, new jobs and social opportunities.	Possible cannibalization effects
Increase the guarantee period	Bonus	Manufacturers, people	Reduction of natural resources usage, extended life cycles	High end-of-use options, medium content value, and medium life cycle	Opportunities for reusing, creating new business opportunities in the second-hand market and new jobs.	Making goods more durable contrasts with the recycling principles, products can be heavier generating higher opex, cannibalization due to products living for longer periods
Favor R&D support for integrated value-chain projects and investment in new circular activities	Bonus	All firms involved in a supply chain	Favor the adoption of circular systems	All configurations of the waste cascade	Promote initiatives along the supply chain, with the purposes of integrating firms' business models, favoring joint investments, and seeking to establish well-functioning circular economy systems	Long procedures to get the funds that may be not in line with social and humanitarian emergencies, the funds can be under-estimated, the implied radical changes may limit its adoption
Set up green deals and clusters at different levels	Bonus	All firms involved in a supply chain	Favor the adoption of circular systems	All configurations of the waste cascade	Promoting the integration among supply chain partners giving rise to industrial symbiosis, industrial ecology, and circular districts.	Long procedures to get the funds that may be not in line with social and humanitarian emergencies, the funds can be under-estimated, the partners can be geographically dispersed

Favor environmental labeling and certification	Bonus	All firms involved in a supply chain	Favor the recognition of circular economy content	All configurations of the waste cascade	The society recognizes the efforts made in terms of circular economy and sustainability, enhancing the value of the brand. This mechanism favors the innovation and the contributions to greening the society.	Investments in methodology and research linked to public data collection and analysis, environmental impact, weighting and framing.
Communication about the repair of products	Bonus	Manufacturers and suppliers	Acknowledge consumers on repair opportunities	Early stage linked to product design and final stages linked to repair and avoid disposal	Extending the product life cycle and decreasing the amount of natural resources used.	Consumers do not replace the goods, generating lower sales. Users must acquire new competences in repairing the goods. Need for a dictionary.
Material taxation	Malus	Suppliers and manufacturers	Reduce the use of hazardous waste	Prevention and reuse	Reduce the societal and environmental impacts of hazardous waste. Favor the use and the reuse of circular content.	Understand and analyze the implications of substituting the hazardous materials with the green materials, like, quality standards and controls, process innovation investments, and modification of the supply chain structure to include new and atypical stakeholders. Negative externalities linked to the price of materials, limiting its accessibility. Taxation may differ from country to country. Repercussions linked to one firm over the entire supply chain.

Modulation of EPR fees	Malus/bonus	Manufacturers	Improve the goods' circularity	Extending the product life cycle	Increase the product usage and extend the product life cycle. Reduce the amount of natural resources and environmental impact linked to making new goods.	Low opportunity to activate product's replacement. The public authority can decide the features according to which the fees should be computed; hence, the firms' decisions are subject to uncertainty.
EPR: adapting contract duration and conditions	Bonus	Manufacturers	Improve the circular system	Supporting the product life cycle	Absorb the risks linked to the EPR.	It requires stable countries and systems.
Green public procurement	Bonus	All stakeholders making purchasing decisions	Favor the adoption of green materials	Procurement tasks of all stages	Support the circularity of products and services, also through ad hoc labels. Investments can have heterogeneous aims, like: reduction of over-packaging, longer product lifecycles, availability of spare parts, and information to consumers.	Adjustments and alignment to the public conditions and frameworks. The users should be educated to raise their circular behaviors and accept higher prices for green products. Circular projects can require long term objectives and targets against the urgent environmental objectives.
Mandatory recycled content	Malus	Suppliers, manufacturers, and recyclers	Reduce the resource consumption to favor the use of recycled materials	All cascade blocks that can use recycle materials	Stimuli for purchasing green materials and the related market. Favor the access to investments and accessibility to new materials.	The recycling materials must be accessible from an economic point of view as well as from a feedstock availability point of view. The presence of recycling materials should not be perceived as low quality of a certain good. Not all countries are in favor of using recycling materials. Needs of new systems to check any possible contamination.

Landfill and incineration ban/tax	Malus	All stakeholders using landfills	Apply circular principles instead of wasting resources	Final stage of the life cycle	Favor the diffusion of circular systems. Increase the health and the living conditions for the society.	Ban and tax amounts are not necessarily fixed upfront but they could be adjusted according to some features, like, make sorting before landfilling or presence of recycling materials. Difficult applications for household waste. Difficulties for stakeholders who cannot implement circular systems.
Waste producers pay the full waste management cost	Malus	All stakeholders making waste	Avoid waste	Final stage of the life cycle	Reduce the waste and all activities required for managing waste. Encourage the adoption of circular systems.	Determine the fees to be applied to the different stakeholders. Difficulties in identifying the stakeholder who is responsible for the waste creation when being in international contexts and/or working in extended supply chains.
Lower VAT on green products and services	Bonus	All stakeholders contributing to circular systems	Favor the adoption of the circular principles	All stages of the life cycle	Encourage stakeholders to adopt circular systems.	The definition of circular good is not given; hence, the percentage of VAT discount to apply is challenging. Difficulties in identifying the stakeholder who is responsible for the waste creation when being in international contexts and/or working in extended supply chains.

Addressing waste exports from the EU	Malus	All stakeholders making hazardous waste and exporting it	Waste reduction	All stages of the life cycle when the waste created is then exported	Waste reduction. Substitution of hazardous waste with green and circular materials. Combat the illegal transport of waste.	Monitoring activities to combat the waste exportation. High investments to shift from hazardous waste to circular materials. The mechanism does not solve the issue of heterogeneous waste.
Tradable recycling credits schemes	Bonus	All stakeholders who can reuse secondary materials	Waste reduction	All stages of the life cycle when the secondary materials can be shown to be reused	Encourage stakeholders to implement circular systems by sponsoring the use and the reuse of secondary material. Reduction of natural resources. Credits to be redeemed or sold.	The credits are difficult to estimate when the materials used are heterogeneous. The credits' value can be subject to market distortions. Regulations do not model the credits' dynamics.
Subsidies	Bonus	All stakeholders undertaking circular economy projects with high risk of failure	All aspects of circular systems	All stages of the life cycle	Support the creation of circular economy systems, even in cases of low appealing frameworks.	Subsidies absorb public funds, which could have been spent elsewhere. No clear identification of features to sponsor circularity (e.g., material substitution vs. packaging lightweight). The subsidy can be proportional to the circular economy project value, whose measure is not uniquely recognized.

Chapter 4

VALUE CREATION AND CAPTURE IN THE CIRCULAR ECONOMY

Pietro De Giovanni

ABSTRACT: *The value that circular economy systems can recover is a joint endeavor between consumers and collectors, which exerts efforts and adopts behavior to ensure the success of circular economy strategies. This chapter describes the importance of consumers' and collectors' roles in preserving the value of waste and describes how responsible behaviors and circular design principles support circular economy systems. Furthermore, it explains how blockchain technology can help circular economies to verify the value of returns and product waste, implying the reengineering of corporate strategy.*

4.1. Value identification and capture through consumers' responsible behaviors

The EUGreenDeal (2021) estimates that over 80% of all product-related environmental impacts are determined during the design phase of a product [1]. Therefore, desires to implement a circular economy system are strongly connected to investments made in product design to improve circularity. Several countries have developed ad-hoc action plans to push firms to design sustainable and more circular goods by reengineering some specific features such as easy to repair and easy to recycle, and by identifying a certain amount of recycled content within the material used. However, firms have faced considerable skepticism by consumers due to possible premature obsolescence of products, low quality when circular content is present, and possible cannibalization effects with other product categories (e.g., a recycled product can cannibalize the primary market).

Indeed, the historical paradigm followed in most businesses is the 'take-

[1] EUGreenDeal (2021). Circular Economy Action Plan. For a cleaner and more competitive Europe. https://ec.europa.eu/environment/pdf/circular-economy/new_circular_economy_action_plan.pdf (Latest access: February 2022).

make-dispose' model, also identified as the 'linear' business model. Therefore, shifting to a circular economy model based on the waste cascade described in Chapter 1 requires a radical change in both consumer behaviors and firms' *modus operandi.* The difficulties linked to this paradigm change are derived from the hidden value behind end-of-life and end-of-use goods. *How can consumers and firms recognize the value of circular content?* So far, the answer to this question has been more theoretical than practical. Various research studies have been sponsored to pursue policies based on awareness, education and competencies, through which people's commitment and willingness to accept and seek out more sustainable consumption linked to environmental and social scopes are bolstered. Therefore, people should be encouraged to increase their sense of responsibility and make behavioral changes by undertaking an educational path from an early age onward to incorporate responsible and sustainable dimensions. Similarly, countless research studies promote the adoption of sustainable and ethical practices for firms, while the real basis for the circular economy lies in the creation of a suitable reverse logistics network to collect content from the market and provide it to the firms (as seen in Chapter 2), and to design goods to be more circular. Therefore, the value linked to the circular economy requires two primary efforts: Consumers, who must be very well informed about the characteristics of the content to return in order to preserve its value, as well as firms, which must invest in product design to guarantee high returns value in the future.

The aim of preserving the value of the circular economy begins with the responsible behavior that consumers adopt, which links to the type of returns to handle, the hazardous content, and the level of recyclability. One worldwide issue that firms, countries, and people must solve is how to manage and treat the plastic. The mass production of polymers and poor control of plastic products at end of life have resulted in a drastic increase of plastic entering the marine environment around the globe[2]. Plastic's durability and density make it transportable over large distances without being damaged, and it persists in the marine eco-system for long time periods. The result is the global contamination of the maritime environment, from remote lakes to the deepest oceans[3]. Besides adopting responsible behaviors, consumers should acquire more knowledge about the circular economy of plastic to make a real and tangible contribution to the eco-system. In fact, a responsible behavior

[2] Welden, N.A. (2020). The environmental impacts of plastic pollution. In *Plastic Waste and Recycling* (pp. 195-222). Academic Press.

[3] Bucci, K., Tulio, M., & Rochman, C.M. (2020). What is known and unknown about the effects of plastic pollution: A meta-analysis and systematic review. *Ecological Applications*, *30*(2).

does not rely on putting the plastic material in a plastic trash receptacle, but, rather, requires an understanding of the type of plastic that is put in the trash. Plastic can be classified into the following categories:

- *Recyclable plastic.* This type of plastic is the outcome of a recycling process, during which the plastic is converted and used for other applications with the purpose of keeping products away from the landfill. While recycling paper or glass is relatively simple for customers, contributing to the recycling of plastic is less straightforward. For example, there are many types of plastic packaging, some commonly recycled, others almost never recyclable (Cozzolino and De Giovanni, 2022)[4]. Dean (2020) identifies a study by Ecover, whose findings highlight that two-thirds of British customers recycle as often as they can; however, 37% admit they don't always know whether a product's packaging can be recycled. Consequently, if circularity is not done properly, the potential value obtainable from recycling is essentially lost.
- *Biodegradable plastic.* When content is biodegradable, it can be broken down naturally by microorganisms such as bacteria, which are activated when the eco-system reaches certain conditions in terms of temperature and humidity. These conditions determine the decomposition time, making biodegradable plastic very challenging for the eco-system, as it may take many years before degradation. In this sense, biodegradable plastic is more eco-friendly since it decomposes much faster than traditional plastic, which may take hundreds of years to break down. The degradation process happens by breaking down the plastic and reducing its dimensions until it dissolves. Although the decomposition process is natural, it can still be harmful to the environment due to methane emissions. Most importantly, the value of recycling load can be harmed when biodegradable plastic enters the traditional recycling process. The recycling system will consider the biodegradable plastic as an impurity, requiring additional sustainable operations to be carried out. Consumers play an important role in properly returning biodegradable plastic, considering that volumes of post-consumer waste are up to five times larger than those generated by the industry[5]. For example, consumers can put together No. 1 and No. 2 plastics. However, putting a biodegradable bag with No. 7 plastic into the same bin contaminates the entire "recyclable" load, consequently losing the value of biodegradables

---

[4] Cozzolino, A., & De Giovanni, P. (2022). The Circular Economy of Packaging: An Analysis of Italian Firms. *International Journal of Logistics Management,* 1-20.

[5] Patel, M., von Thienen, N., Jochem, E., & Worrell, E. (2000). Recycling of plastics in Germany. *Resour., Conserv. Recycling*, *29*, 65-90.

as well as impacting the value of recyclables, which require additional operations. This is because the different density of biodegradable plastics requires expensive adjustments in waste collection and treatment.

- *Bio-plastics*. Similarly to biodegradable plastic, bio-plastics are not intended for recycling processes and should not be mixed with traditional plastic waste. Otherwise, they can contaminate and disrupt the recycling stream, deteriorating the value of the recycling material. Bio-plastics are made from natural resources and materials such as starch, corn, potato, and tapioca starches, cellulose, soy protein, and lactic acid. Therefore, at the end of the life cycle, they decompose fully into the eco-system without producing toxic residue. A typical application of bio-plastics is compostable plastic, which degrades by at least 90% in weight in six months in an environment rich in carbon dioxide. At least 90% of the mass of the selected material must be reduced to fragments of less than 2 mm if in contact with organic materials for a period of three months, the presence of the material must not cause negative effects on the composting process, and the amount of heavy metals present in the composted material must not exceed specified standards[6]. However, consumers who collect compostable plastic and return it through circular economy systems should pay attention to whether the compostable goods are suitable for home composting. In terms of value, compostable plastic is made from plants instead of petrochemicals derived from fossil fuels. Consequently, it uses less energy and generates less green gas emissions. However, consumer utility can be seriously harmed by compostable goods usage, which must be stored at a certain temperature, away from heat sources and sunlight. Bioplastics are not necessarily compostable or biodegradable. For example, a polylactic acid (PLA) bioplastic is biodegradable, whereas a polyethene terephthalate (PET) bioplastic is not. The latter is consequently (only) recyclable, highlighting the possible mistakes and confusion the label "bio" can cause among consumers.

The previous discussion about the importance of responsible behavior in plastic collection is much broader and involves all types of circular content that people manage. The need to pursue a global circular economy perspective and the related engagement come from the continuous reduction of the natural resources available around the globe, which is exacerbated by a drastic increase in the population and industrial activities. In fact, consumers should adopt responsible behaviors by contributing to the

---

[6] Calabrò, P.S., & Grosso, M. (2018). Bioplastics and waste management. *Waste Management*, *78*, 800-801.

circularity of any type of waste materials (e.g., paper, wood, metals), as well as waste from durable goods (e.g., furniture, electronics, vehicles). This requires important cultural changes and adjustments of consumers' habits, which need to be aligned to circular economy systems. In the literature, a habit is defined as a "behavior repeated over time", which leads to better predictability of that behavior [7], is measured by past behaviors, and seeks to maintain the habit in the future [8]. Accordingly, the willingness to adopt more sustainable behaviors can lead to an improved society and, consequently, a willingness to change old behavior can affect intention and the uptake of behaviors inspired by circular economy targets [9]. Indeed, this shift becomes possible only when consumers acquire a certain attitude about the environment, which is described as consumer awareness of current environmental issues and their feelings of guilt over the human-caused nature of these issues [10]. As empirically demonstrated by Elzinga et al. (2020), consumers who disregard circular economy systems do not perceive their environmental benefits and consequently do not possess environmental attitudes when determining their intention toward a certain circular economy practice [11]. Therefore, firms offering a circular economy should sponsor the environmental and social benefits of circular systems to enhance consumer awareness and acceptance, which will then lead to consumers' intentions toward circular behaviors. These changes are fundamental to enable the process of value capture in the circular economy.

4.2. Value creation and conservation through circular design

The concept of eco-design, also known as design for the environment, has gained increasing attention over various decades. In 1990, Hewlett–Packard implemented a design for the environment program to decrease products' environmental impact in terms of material usage and energy con-

---

[7] Verplanken, B., & Holland, R.W. (2002). Motivated decision making: Effects of activation and self-centrality of values on choices and behavior. *Journal of Personality and Social Psychology*, *82*(3), 434.

[8] Harich, J. (2010). Change resistance as the crux of the environmental sustainability problem. *System Dynamics Review*, *26*(1), 35-72.

[9] Elzinga, R., Reike, D., Negro, S.O., & Boon, W.P. (2020). Consumer acceptance of circular business models. *Journal of Cleaner Production*, *254*, 119988.

[10] Bamberg, S., & Möser, G. (2007). Twenty years after Hines, Hungerford, and Tomera: A new meta-analysis of psycho-social determinants of pro-environmental behaviour. *Journal of Environmental Psychology*, *27*(1), 14-25.

[11] Elziga et al. (2020). *Ibidem*.

sumption [12]. The main strategies for eco-design are as follows: Using materials with low environmental impact, choosing clean production processes, avoiding hazardous and toxic materials, maximizing the efficiency of the energy used for production and for the product in use, and designing for waste management and recycling [13]. A design for the environment program seeks to optimize the interactions between the economic system and the environmental system in order to bridge sustainable development goals and firms' targets [14]. Therefore, customers, suppliers, laboratories, as well as environmental and governmental agencies all have a specific role in transforming design for the environment strategies into real and concrete actions [15].

The design-for-environment principles applied to circular economy systems translate into circular design principles, which are exemplified by the chance to apply the various blocks of the waste cascade during the life cycle, focusing on "reduction, reuse, and recycling" as driving principles inspired by value creation and conservation. Specifically, the circular design aims to create value by making goods that can contribute to feedstock creation and that conserve their value for the longest possible time period. To achieve these targets, product designers should rethink the product from the beginning by adopting circular criteria as a starting point: For example, by reengineering the logistics and production processes to accommodate circularity principles, shaping regenerative life cycles to reach sustainability targets, and making goods that can be easily repaired, reused, recycled or transformed. Regarding the circular design of electronics, the materials embedded in the goods should be designed and selected to conserve their value and possible future applications, also in domains that are atypical and far from the original application. According to the Circular Design Guide, sponsored by the MacArthur Foundation in collaboration with IDEO [16], the principles of circular design are as follows:

- *Understand.* Firms should invest in training and knowledge regarding

[12] Tischner, U., & Hora, M. (2019). Sustainable electronic product design. In *Waste electrical and electronic equipment (WEEE) handbook* (pp. 443-482). Woodhead Publishing.

[13] Ljungberg, L.Y. (2007). Materials selection and design for development of sustainable products. *Materials & Design*, *28*(2), 466-479.

[14] Sun, J., Han, B., Ekwaro-Osire, S., & Zhang, H.C. (2003). Design for environment: Methodologies, tools, and implementation. *Journal of Integrated Design and Process Science*, 7(1), 59-75.

[15] Maranesi, C., & De Giovanni, P. (2020). Modern circular economy: Corporate strategy, supply chain, and industrial symbiosis. *Sustainability*, *12*(22), 9383.

[16] https://www.iberdrola.com/social-commitment/circular-design.

the different circular design solutions that exist for their products and evaluate all available options to successfully move from a linear model to a circular system.

- *Define*. The identification of a possible circular path must be followed by establishing targets and objectives. Because they are linked to sustainability, circular economy strategies can have a broad scope and involve stakeholders at various levels and in different life cycle stages. According to the circular design, the economic value to be extracted from each life cycle phase takes dynamic forms.
- *Make*. The implementation of a successful circular economy system requires an alignment between the targets and a full understanding of the system's potential, which are given by the consumers' willingness to close the loops and the presence of adequate reverse logistics systems. The combination of such ingredients allows firms to develop both proof of concepts and circular economy prototypes, with the aim of identifying the circular network.
- *Launch*. The identified circular economy is released and put into practice. Monitoring activities supply feedback on the circular economy's effectiveness and create the basis for continuous system improvements.

Indeed, along with the monetary value, circular design guarantees several environmental benefits. Circular design enables the minimization of resource consumption due to the value conservation principles behind it. Accordingly, it leads to a natural reduction of waste, emissions, and pollution. Since the circular design improves product circularity over the entire life cycle, it grants a lower utilization of natural resources like energy and water, due to the reduced amount of operations and treatment to be carried out when closing the loop and resulting in optimized production and logistics systems. A circular design seeks durable and resistant materials and goods aimed at extending the useful life of products. Considering all of these features, products made using circular design principles receive recognition from society for the protection of biodiversity and the battle against global warming.

Because circular systems involve many processes and supply chain actors, the circular design must be complemented by investments and supplier selection processes created ad hoc. Among the practices to be included in the circular design, the EU (2014) pays specific attention to the following[17]: *Lightening,* the reduction of raw materials to provide a particular service; *dura-*

[17] EU (2014). Towards a circular economy: A zero waste programme for Europe. http://hytechcycling.eu/wp-content/uploads/Towards-a-circular-economy-A-zero-waste-programme-for-Europe.pdf.

bility, prolonging the useful life of the products; *efficacy,* reducing energy and material consumption in phases of production and use; *replacement,* reducing the use of hazardous or difficult to recycle materials in products or production processes; *recycled material*, creating secondary raw material markets (based on standards, public procurement, etc.); *eco-design,* designing products that are easier to maintain, repair, upgrade, process or recycle; *regeneration,* developing necessary services for users such as maintenance and repair services; *consumer-based incentives,* stimulating and supporting waste reduction and high-quality separate collection by consumers; *collector-based incentives*, stimulating separation and collection systems that minimize both recycling and reuse costs; *industrial symbiosis,* facilitating the grouping of cluster activities in order to prevent the by-products from being converted into waste; *social development*, promoting wider and better choices for consumers through hiring, borrowing or sharing services as an alternative to product ownership, while protecting the interests of consumers (in terms of costs, protection, information, contractual terms, insurance aspects, etc.).

Sumter et al. (2020) make use of the set of competences [18] identified by Wiek et al. (2011) to identify design systems, concepts, and methods for the circular economy [19]. Accordingly, firms can fully exploit the circular economy's potential when acquiring design capabilities, which are given by the following:

- *Systems thinking competency* is the ability to collectively analyze complex systems across different domains (society, environment, economy, etc.) and across different scales (local to global);
- *Anticipatory competency* is the ability to collectively analyze, evaluate, and craft rich 'pictures' of the future related to sustainability issues and sustainability problem-solving frameworks;
- *Normative competency* is the ability to collectively map, specify, apply, reconcile, and negotiate sustainability values, principles, goals, and targets;
- *Strategic competency* is the ability to collectively design and implement interventions, transitions, and transformative governance strategies toward sustainability;
- *Interpersonal competency* is the ability to facilitate collaborative and par-

---

[18] Sumter, D., de Koning, J., Bakker, C., & Balkenende, R. (2020). Circular economy competencies for design. *Sustainability*, *12*(4), 1561.

[19] Wiek, A., Withycombe, L., & Redman, C.L. (2011). Key competencies in sustainability: A reference framework for academic program development. *Sustainability Science*, *6*(2), 203-218.

ticipatory problem solving, while ensuring a respectful and empathetic exchange of perspectives and actions and dealing with conflict resolution.

By acquiring all of these competences, circular economy systems are then able to apply circular design principles to the life cycle assessment and determine the total environmental impacts by developing one unique framework.

4.3. Unlocking circular economy value through blockchain

Several public policies and firms' take-back programs strive to give consumers the right knowledge regarding benefits and opportunities gained when contributing to circular economy systems, also including environmental and social outcomes. However, to increase consumers' participation in the circular economy and make them more knowledgeable about the circular economy's potential, several legislative and public actions have been changed and improved in that direction. In other words, consumers should receive trustworthy and relevant information on products, independent of purchasing in a store or online, including their lifespan, the materials used, the processes, and many other pieces of information which can also be product-specific[20]. Among the various policies, consumer protection is pursued by verifying any possible green washing issues, setting compulsory requirements for sustainability such as labels and logos, and connecting consumers to informational tools. The need to be visible and transparent clearly has the objective of making people aware of the real benefits of the circular economy and sustainable practices, which can otherwise remain as simple attempts rather than real actions. In the modern business models and circular economy systems, blockchain is the digital technology that simultaneously enables all of these targets.

In fact, among the general properties of blockchain technology, circular economy systems can manage circular content transparency, verify the originality of collected material, ensure the traceability of waste and recycled content, and consequently mitigate business, environmental and social risks linked to circular economy systems. The blockchain unlocks the value of circular content by collecting pieces of information from the eco-system and recording them in an immutable dataset, which is then available to firms, consumers, governments, and all stakeholders. To pursue such targets, a blockchain uses a set of digital applications to track, trace, and verify

[20] EUGreenDeal (2021). *Ibidem.*

how the waste move along a territory and across a closed loop supply chain, from the waste producer to the waste facility. The blockchain allows each stakeholder access to updated information regarding the status of the waste material and records all transactions relative to the waste and product life cycles. Therefore, blockchain monitors the actions of firms, consumers, suppliers and collectors and activates smart contracts, including the incentives introduced in Chapters 2 and 3 [21].

Today, circular economy systems are geographically extended and dispersed, making the boundaries of a closed-loop system difficult to identify and monitor [22]. Along with the management of relationships emerging from the circular economy, firms are challenged by several worldwide inefficiencies, including transactions costs, regulatory constraints, waste contamination, possible unethical practices and routines used when collecting goods, the use of environmentally harmful processes for collecting, transporting and treating the material waste, cultural barriers and language differences, the need to align transportation strategies according to regulations and legislative constraints, and a lack of trust and commitment among consumers and collectors when they play a role in enhancing the visibility, transparency, and verifiability of the circular content. Blockchain technology enables trustless networking, because the parties can make transactions even though they do not trust each other; hence, it favors the movement of waste material even without checking its content through the traditional quality check procedures currently used in several business contexts [23].

The scientific literature has already well-documented the benefits of using blockchain in the circular economy. Recent works highlight how blockchain can provide several advantages for the circular economy [24-25]. In particular, the features of traceability and transparency that blockchain ensures by recording information about the circular economy lead to enhanced optimiza-

---

[21] De Giovanni, P. (2019). Eco-digital supply chains through blockchains. *International Journal of Business and Management Study*. 6, 2.

[22] De Giovanni, P. (2022). Leveraging the Circular Economy with Closed-loop Supply Chain and Reverse Omni-channel using Blockchain Technology and Incentives. *International Journal of Operations and Production Management*, 42(7), 959-994.

[23] De Giovanni, P. (2021). Smart Contracts and Blockchain for Supply Chain Quality Management. In *Dynamic Quality Models and Games in Digital Supply Chains* (pp. 91-110). Springer, Cham.

[24] Kouhizadeh, M., Sarkis, J., & Zhu, Q. (2019). At the nexus of blockchain technology, the circular economy, and product deletion. *Applied Sciences*, *9*(8), 1712.

[25] Bekrar, A., El Cadi, A.A., Todosijevic, R., & Sarkis, J. (2021). Digitalizing the closing-of-the-loop for supply chains: A transportation and Blockchain perspective. *Sustainability*, *13*(5), 2895.

tion of the entire system. Inspired by the worldwide effects of COVID-19, Nandi et al. (2021) investigate the possible responses that a blockchain enabled circular economy can provide to supply chain problems and issues that have emerged during the pandemic[26]. Several business aspects are analyzed, and different possible practices are proposed in a theoretical and conceptual framework. Böckel et al. (2021) carry out a review of blockchain studies in a circular economy and find a mismatch between theory and practice when blockchain is applied to the circular economy[27]. The authors highlight that although the potential for blockchain can be very helpful in a circular economy, questions must still be resolved regarding whether blockchain can accelerate the move toward a circular economy.

In the literature on closed-loop supply chains and the circular economy, De Giovanni et al. (2016) and De Giovanni (2018) proposed a contract that is called an incentive mechanism[28-29], according to which supply chain members are penalized economically every time one deviates from the optimal strategies defined by the vertical integrated solution. While this remains a theoretical exercise, the blockchain offers the chance to make this framework executable through smart contracts. For example, in a traditional transaction, a seller sells one ton of recycled plastic to a buyer, by guaranteeing a certain level of purity and quality of the recycling material. In a traditional framework, the transaction of money from the buyer to the seller occurs before the buyer receives the recycling material from the seller; that is, the financial transaction occurs without that the buyer verifies the quality of the recycling materials. Afterwards, when the delivery is finalized and the buyer receives the goods, possible quality and nonconformity issues linked to the recycling material require the activation of a complaint process, which should lead to the parties' reconciliation. In contrast, when using blockchain, the buyer does not pay the seller when they place the order; rather, a certain amount of digital assets from the buyer's wallet are

---

[26] Nandi, S., Sarkis, J., Hervani, A.A., & Helms, M.M. (2021). Redesigning supply chains using blockchain-enabled circular economy and COVID-19 experiences. *Sustainable Production and Consumption*, *27*, 10-22.

[27] Böckel, A., Nuzum, A.K., & Weissbrod, I. (2021). Blockchain for the circular economy: Analysis of the research-practice gap. *Sustainable Production and Consumption*, *25*, 525-539.

[28] De Giovanni, P., Reddy, P.V., & Zaccour, G. (2016). Incentive strategies for an optimal recovery program in a closed-loop supply chain. *European Journal of Operational Research*, *249*(2), 605-617.

[29] De Giovanni, P. (2018). A joint maximization incentive in closed-loop supply chains with competing retailers: The case of spent-battery recycling. *European Journal of Operational Research*, *268*(1), 128-147.

frozen when the seller sends the goods. The amount is then unlocked when the delivery is finalized and after the buyer has checked the quality of the goods received and verified the level of purity of the recycling material. According to the real performance of the seller, the buyer will then decide to pay the seller by unlocking the amount from its wallet or simply reject the recycled content received.

Used in this way, blockchain can substantially help the circular economy system to demonstrate and verify the real benefits obtainable. To do so, all technology features must be actionable and controllable by using oracles, such that the buyer's information is verified and recorded on the blockchain, while the machine learning algorithm behind the blockchain activates the smart contracts accordingly. Through these mechanisms, all parties have incentives to stick to the contractual terms. Indeed, the most precious work is done by the oracles. To execute a smart contract, the blockchain needs access to external data through the oracles present within the eco-system, which connect the physical world with the digital world, allowing individuals to verify and authenticate the smart contract clauses as well as to pursue its execution. The oracles can be classified into *software oracles*, which gather data and information from online sources (e.g., Google maps, the Financial Times) and feed them into smart contracts, *hardware oracles*, which provide data from physical devices dispersed over a certain territory and generally serve other purposes (e.g., home sensors and video devices), *human oracles*, which refer to a network of people physically present within the eco-system who can verify some information to reach a consensus if they are connected to the blockchain system, *inbound oracles*, which are offline sources of information that go from the eco-system to the blockchain and that are recorded somewhere, and *outbound oracles*, which are offline sources of information going from the blockchain to the eco-system.

Using this framework, blockchain records information on the entire history of goods circulating around the world, recording all information relative to life cycle to be accessed by consumers, firms, and suppliers using a simple tag and platforms. Therefore, blockchain can collect and record information at each stage of the return process within circular economy systems and make it available to society at large. As has emerged from the literature review, although there is clear evidence of the positive effects induced by the circular economy to the eco-system and society at large, the key topic that must still be addressed is how firms can engage consumers and collectors in contributing to the system's circularity. In fact, without responsible and conscious behaviors to collect information, the circular economy system will never acquire a sufficient feedstock for the efficient management of circular activities. The blockchain can then be the technology through which firms can move from a passive to an active approach to returns.

As mentioned in Chapter 2, in the passive return approach, also referred to as the waste-stream approach, collection happens on a voluntary basis, and the circular economy system is primarily considered a cost center; therefore, neither firms nor consumers that are part of the circular economy system receive any incentive to close the loop. Rather, they are motivated by their own responsible sentiment and willingness to preserve the environment for future generations. In contrast, an active return approach, also referred to as a value-stream approach, implies that the circular economy system is managed as a value-creation center, through which collectors and consumers involved in the collection process receive a reward as a counterpart for their responsible actions. Therefore, whoever collects information is actively incentivized to undertake responsible behaviors.

Interestingly, when circular systems make use of an active return approach, the blockchain can activate smart contracts in both cases of consumer and collector incentives. By using inbound and outbound oracles, as well as software, hardware, and human oracles, the smart contracts activate incentives for both consumers and collectors when they have performed as written in the smart clauses[30]. The integration including blockchain, the circular economy, and incentives represents a revolution in the creation and management of circular systems and can be an effective way to increase the feedstock. As explained in Table 1, the blockchain technology can activate a value-stream approach that is composed of a dual incentive, one for consumers and one for collectors. This happens only when the algorithm behind it is written according to clauses and conditions linked to the performance of both consumers and collectors. On the one hand, consumers adopting responsible behavior gain benefits given by fidelity points, cryptocurrency, or tokens. On the other hand, collectors performing in accordance with the contract terms receive payment, also in terms of cryptocurrency or tokens. The same type of reasoning applies to deviating behavior. For example, when a consumer does not behave responsibly, the blockchain records that information, and the smart contract can either reduce his or her wallet by a certain amount or decrease the gain that the consumer was supposed to receive in the next transaction. Similarly, when a collector does not respect the delivery time written in the contract, it can receive

---

[30] De Giovanni, P. (2022). Blockchain Technology Applications in Businesses and Organizations. IGI Global, Hershey PA.

a lower payment or a reduction in tokens or cryptocurrency. In this sense, the blockchain can manage either fungible or non-fungible tokens. Their difference consists of the content to which they refer. An example of fungible tokens is Bitcoin, for which the owner can recognize a certain value, which is divisible and possibly used for other transactions: The fungible tokens can then be easily used to activate smart contracts in the circular economy and engage both collectors and consumers. In contrast, the non-fungible tokens store a value that is not divisible and recognizable elsewhere. In general, the nonfungible tokens store data such as an academic title or artwork, which are not divisible. Therefore, the nonfungible tokens can be applied to verify and improve the circular economic content's transactions, like bulks of recycled paper or plastic.

As explained in Table 1, the blockchain technology can also be used to activate partially active return approaches. This is for a case in which only one between the consumers and collectors is subject to incentives implemented and managed through smart contracts. Indeed, the choice depends on many factors including integration with the oracles (e.g., it may be difficult to capture single consumer behaviors through oracles and determine whether or not it is responsible), the transaction costs (e.g., since the value of the return can be low, the level of transaction costs can either limit or favor the blockchain adoption), or the collection of content (e.g., managing waste in remote regions in which 4G does not work makes blockchain ineffective).

Table 1. Theoretical framework with circular economy system, blockchain, and incentives.

	Collector incentives	**No collector incentives**
Consumer incentives	**Value-stream approach** The circular economy system engages in an active return (value-stream) approach. The blockchain activates the smart contracts based on both consumer and collector incentives.	**Consumer-based value-stream approach** The circular economy system engages in a partially active return approach by focusing on consumer incentives. The blockchain activates the smart contracts according to consumer incentives.
No consumer incentives	**Collector-based value-stream approach** The circular economy system engages in a partially active return approach by focusing on collector incentives. The blockchain activates the smart contracts according to collector incentives.	**Waste-stream approach** The circular economy system does not engage either consumers or collectors in the collection or production, being de facto passive. The blockchain does not activate the smart contracts based on incentives.

4.4. New strategies for value creation in the circular economy

The new circular economy paradigm has important implications for the firms' functional and corporate strategies. The entire business model and supply chain network of relationships can undergo radical changes when undertaking circular principles. The literature on the circular economy and professionals' experiences in the field suggest a series of classifications of the business models to include under the umbrella of circular economy to ensure the proper extraction of value. Five areas of intervention exist in this framework[31-32]: 1. *Sales model*, in which the circular economy requires the identification of possible markets in which to position goods after their first life; without an appropriate sales model analysis, any circular economy project is destined to fail; 2. *Product design and material composition*, as explained in Section 4.2, which allows the circular economy to achieve its targets; 3. *IT and data management*, in which the circular economy requires the adaptation of the information system that must handle the reverse flows and keep track of products, components, and material data; 4. *Closed-loop*, in which the forward and reverse logistics flows should be integrated and optimized to acquire value from products, components, and materials flows; 5. *Strategic relationships*, in which the circular economy requires trusted partnerships and long-term relationships with suppliers and customers, including new processes like co-creation and co-design; 6. *Incentives*, in which the circular economy requires new habits by consumers and collectors to be acquired through training programs and rewards.

Within these frameworks, the scientific literature and the professional world have identified new strategies that firms can adopt in the circular economy, which are: Circular inputs, sharing platforms, product as a service, product life extension, product use extension, resource recovery.

Circular inputs

The circular inputs strategy focuses on the raw materials used in production. The new paradigms linked to the circular economy push firms to adopt renewable resources and abandon wasted resources since these are source of sustainable impacts. Examples of wasted resources are single-use material and toxic material. While modern firms' strategies seek to reach zero-waste and zero-emissions targets, the adoption of circular inputs strat-

---

[31] Laubscher, M., & Marinelli, T. (2014, November). Integration of circular economy in business. In *Proceedings of the Conference: Going Green – Care Innovation* (pp. 1-7).

[32] Lewandowski, M. (2016). Designing the business models for circular economy—Towards the conceptual framework. *Sustainability*, *8*(1), 43.

egies can go beyond them since the renewable resources can favor some natural processes. The best sustainable technologies are the ones leading to industrial ecology, through which the waste mimics the eco-system, like photosynthesis. National Geographic describes photosynthesis as the process through which "*...plants take in carbon dioxide (CO_2) and water (H_2O) from the air and soil. Within the plant cell, the water is oxidized, meaning it loses electrons, while the carbon dioxide is reduced, meaning it gains electrons. This transforms the water into oxygen and the carbon dioxide into glucose. The plant then releases the oxygen back into the air, and stores energy within the glucose molecules*".

According to Mohsenpour et al. (2021), several companies take the waste-water coming from industrial activities and use it to raise algae by exploiting photosynthesis; the result is a purified water that goes back to industrial applications while generating new inputs (algae) for the ecosystem [33]. Considering this framework in a more general discussion, the circular inputs strategy seeks to engage firms in using renewable, recycled, or highly recyclable inputs to enable either the partial or total elimination of waste and pollution or, in the most successful of cases, reaching resource-additive outcomes. As explained by Lacy et al. (2020), possible solutions applicable in this framework are as follows [34]:

- *Renewable resources,* which offer the dual benefit of developing new bio-based products and decreasing dependence on petroleum products, creating positive effects in the environment through their capacity to restore atmospheric carbon dioxide. The general inputs used in production facilities can be easily and naturally replaced, while the resources can be infinitely used, such as, for example, water from rain or wind and solar energy.
- *Renewable bio-based materials* are materials developed from chemistry derived from living organisms; hence, they are biocompatible, non-toxic, and non-immunogenic, as they derived from organic sources such as cereal, corn, potato, rice, soy, sugar cane, wheat, vegetable oil, etc. Bio-based materials – more than other types of materials – experience a wide range of challenges that can affect their performance, like weathering and moisture. Furthermore, because bio-based materials are organic, they can be attacked by natural organisms such as bacteria, fungi, or insects.

---

[33] Mohsenpour, S.F., Hennige, S., Willoughby, N., Adeloye, A., & Gutierrez, T. (2021). Integrating micro-algae into wastewater treatment: A review. *Science of The Total Environment*, *752*, 142168.

[34] Lacy, P., Long, J., & Spindler, W. (2020). The Circular Business Models. In *The Circular Economy Handbook* (pp. 17-42). Palgrave Macmillan.

- *Renewable man-made materials* are materials based on non-organic chemistry, which can be infinitely recycled without a substantial loss of properties while being more durable and of high quality. Man-made materials, on the other hand, go through rigorous processing to alter the material so that it suits its intended purpose, and as a result, they are not environmentally friendly. For example, polyester has significant negative environmental impacts during production and disposal. On the other hand, it is more sustainable during the usage phase since polyester lasts a long time and requires less water, energy and heat for washing.

The final adoption of a circular inputs strategy requires a comprehensive evaluation of all possible emerging trade-offs. Clearly, the more inputs are eco-friendly and can be suitably used in the circular economy, the more technological development is needed to guarantee cost reduction and a final acceptance by the market. These barriers are present for both renewable energy applications and material input substitution.

The most relevant challenge that circular economy projects face when aimed at circular inputs relates to the complexity of implementing these sustainable solutions. It might be possible that in retaining traditional supply and procurement procedures, as well as methods for selection, the right suppliers are more effective and face less risk than adopting circular materials. The changes in the business models must be carefully tested and analyzed since the learning experiences can be fully lost. In contrast, the circular inputs provide true contributions to the environment by reducing the overall impact and enhancing the firms' reputation and green brand value, which is highly important for today's consumers when making purchasing decisions. Furthermore, purchasing circular material can sometimes be less expensive than purchasing virgin material; for example, the recycling process for plastic can be somewhat expensive, while the output can have economic value. These trade-offs leave room for reflections for firms looking into these avenues.

Sharing platform

The sharing platform strategy allows for the injection of resources within the eco-system to favor circularity through the use of digital applications. The latter are the driving ingredients of this strategy, which presupposes the creation of a platform on which resources are made available and potential users can access them. The main aim of the sharing platforms is to increase and maximize the utilization rates of resources by allowing stakeholders to access the platform and make use of inputs in a convenient way. Therefore, the sharing platform strategy can be easily implemented in all cases in which the capex is high and ownership is not appealing.

Indeed, the sharing platform requires an accurate analysis of the market and the needs to be covered since access to the resources implies that users must be physically near the input location. The business model analysis starts by matching the availability of access to some unused inputs, with a willingness to share unused inputs. Hence, as previously mentioned in Chapter 2, there is a need for users to change habits and receive incentives to use sharing-thinking rather than owning-thinking. By doing so, the circular economy reaches the goal of exploiting the current value of resources (e.g., reusing the current inputs available) and saving virgin materials rather than making and injecting new inputs into the eco-system.

While the sharing platform business model promotes collaboration among users for underutilized assets and resources, the way users employ them remains the main issue. In principle, a firm promoting the circular economy through a sharing platform never becomes the owner of the goods; rather, it plays the role of intermediary between assets and users. However, issues induced by an erroneous use of assets require the platform's owner to reconcile the parties. Regarding the social implications, the use of sharing platforms by people can also be met with reluctance when the product ownership provides recognition from the community and a sense of personal success. In such cases, the circular economy option will not be a feasible model.

An interesting paradox, namely, the regulatory paradox, can exist relative to the use of sharing platforms. On the one hand, sharing platforms are not well-regulated. People and society at large are educated and culturally prepared to adopt sharing options while the regulations are slow in providing norms and rules to adjust behaviors. The unregulated business of city scooters in Europe is an example, since cities become full of scooters affecting traffic and the management of scooter stock over the cities, creating a general risky feeling in pedestrians and drivers. On the other hand, the absence of regulations makes access to and management of the platform very easy and friendly; firms do not have restrictions to follow and do not need to report anything to the public authorities, making the overall business model light and agile. Having no expenses to fulfill regulatory requirements, firms have lower overhead, which contributes toward lowering expenses and keeping platform assets affordable.

Sharing platforms can indeed generate non-monetary value, such as brand recognition and reputation, also serving as effective attractors of funds and subsidies. Sharing platforms can also be considered as a practice to complement the business model with resources and options not available at the current set of assets.

Product as a service

Unlike the sharing platforms, the product as a service business model implies that firms retain the ownership of an asset and gain from the services associated with it, which mainly link to the asset's availability to users. As a counterpart, the asset operations, for example, maintenance and treatments, are still managed and fully paid for by firms. Hence, the assets made circular within the eco-system are always working and well-functioning, while they require incentives linked to durability and upgrades to keep asset performance at consistently high levels.

In most cases, consumers can access a product by subscribing to either a leasing contract or a pay-for-use contract. The circular principles directly apply to consumers who constantly access the asset, increasing the number and the frequency of touchpoints. Indeed, word-of-mouth effects can be easily generated through services, leading to a quick increase in the social networking. The literature has shown the impact of social networks on consumers' willingness to access such solutions, as well as the role the quality of services plays in mitigating possible cases of unsatisfied consumers[35].

Furthermore, the product as a service model has given rise to a new field of study and business applications called "servitization", which link to the general idea that business models are built on the value creation linked to services rather than to the value of the products themselves. Servitization is a crucial aspect in the circular economy considering that circularity starts when firms activate reverse logistics activities; hence, the circular economy can be initiated when the collecting services are well designed, and through which the whole system is competitive: Competition can be played out in product collection, inducing atypical competition based on collecting services. Since the product as a service entails the dematerialization of goods, it turns out not to be risky for consumers who become, at the same time, more exigent and easily shift to competitors' offers.

When analyzing the environmental impacts, a product as a service allows firms to increase profitability by reducing the number of production cycles while focusing on other aspects of the business model such as quality, reliability, performance, and durability. From an economic point of view, the circular model ensures the circulation of single goods that, any time they are sold as services, generate revenues. Since the services are much more affordable than investments in goods, firms can access consumers who are not generally part of their' portfolio. On the other end of the spectrum, firms must

[35] Vessal, S.R., De Giovanni, P., & Hassanzadeh, A. (2021). Technology and service investments in the presence of feature fatigue and word-of-mouth. *European Journal of Operational Research*. 301(3), 923-941.

take and absorb the entire risk of opex and capex. For example, the circular economy would not be effective if the cost of maintenance or the cost of repair is higher than the cost of replacing the goods.

Product life extension

While the circular economy is always thought of as a business model to recover and give new life to waste, recent applications of circular principles focusing on prevention sponsor the adoption of a product life extension business model. The latter applies to all businesses that involve durable goods for which the life cycle can be extended by maximizing both the lifespan and utilization. Additionally, assets that are built on refurbishing, repairing and remanufacturing are examples of the product life extension business model. This option is diametrically opposed to business models based on programmed obsolescence and rapid obsolescence, which aim at pushing consumers to replace their products for new and improved releases. The whole proof-of-concept of product life extension relies on the amount of resources required to make goods and flows going to the landfill. On the one hand, the problem of scarce natural resources pushes governments and firms to value the current stock of available resources and exploit them for as long as possible. On the other hand, extending product life ensures a lower amplitude of end-of-use goods that go to landfills, which are already saturated. Therefore, product life extension seeks to compel users to return durable goods when they reach the end-of-life stage rather than when they reach the end-of-use stage.

Indeed, product life extension comes with some business challenges. Several firms that are well known for their investments in continuous improvement programs, digitalization, and R&D may damage their reputations when extending the product life cycle. Furthermore, revenues generated through the replacement of goods are basically lost. From an operational perspective, the life extension requires that goods are properly designed to guarantee cheap repair and maintenance, while carefully managing the convenience of changing a part of the durable good over the entire product. Instead, from an environmental perspective, a circular economy with product life extension ensures less needs for input along with less waste in the landfill, as well as savings in terms of energy, water, and all natural resources used in production.

Product use extension

Product use extension reverses the pattern of waste management and promotes an image of corporate social responsibility by focusing on the benefits of reusing resources. To be suitable for extensive use, the products must be designed to be repaired, reconditioned, refurbished, or upgraded. Extending the use is economically feasible when a market for such types of goods exists, and when firms possess the capabilities to sell goods in the secondary market while avoiding cannibalization effects. In fact, consumers can play strategically and wait for a new version to be released to purchase the previous version at either a discounted price or directly from the secondary market. Regarding the core market, consumers need to perceive that the current goods are as effective as new releases in satisfying their needs. Very often, durable goods are only marginally updated when new releases are introduced in the market and basic needs can be equally satisfied with both versions. The restyling of a car is a well-fitting example, and it may imply simple adjustments in the vehicle design and aesthetic. To be successful, the product use extension strategy must be followed with a comprehensive marketing plan that considers all emerging side effects of the circular economy.

Resource recovery

Resource recovery consists of converting waste into secondary raw materials to obtain resources, avoid the use of virgin material and natural resources, and decrease the need for waste management. Circular economy systems based on resource recovery require a deep analysis of the recovering options by evaluating the materials used, the production steps, and the product life cycle. Indeed, the recovery option begins when the product reaches the end-of-life stage, implying that it has no market value, and no consumer segment is attracted by its content. In general, the resource recovery option has considerable implications on the quality of the new material obtained through recycling (see Chapter 1), which constrains the possible applications that can be directly connected to the quality of new goods. Therefore, firms pay attention to the resource recovery option since it basically requires limited incremental innovation investments, can easily be integrated within the waste management strategy, links to a sure feedstock in the belief that waste is simply a normal outcome of production, generates direct financial benefits in terms of less resources to purchase, and implies indirect benefits when closing the loop translates into responsible behavior. One clear insight emerges from the resource recovery option: The more firms make waste, the more this solution can be adopted. Hence, industrial applications like oil and gas extraction and treatment, which generate conspicuous amounts of waste, are good candidates for circular economy projects.

While the six proposed options allow firms to create a circular economy, they are not mutually exclusive. Hence, firms can easily combine them to create a multi-objective circular economy system.

Chapter 5
THE SMART CIRCULAR ECONOMY

Pietro De Giovanni

ABSTRACT: *This chapter introduces the concept of the smart circular economy. The adoption of digital technologies and modern managerial paradigms allows circular economy systems to be engineered as intelligent and proactive entities that receive information from the eco-system through digital tools and objects and translate it into knowledge to improve the decision-making process. Hence, a smart circular economy enables circular knowledge.*

5.1. Responsible digitalization through a smart circular economy

As already seen in Chapter 4, a circular economy requires modifications in the industrial paradigms, moving from linear systems to business models on product/service systems, which promote a focused shift away from selling traditional products to offering utilities and services also linked to the collection of waste [1]. Within this new industrial paradigm, a circular economy is believed to have a strong connection with information and knowledge spread over closed loop supply chains. However, the links between the circular economy and traditional information systems are very weak. For example, enterprise resource planning (ERP) has always been used to integrate companies on a global scale but without including the reverse logistics flows, except for some specific applications as the return of pallets or some durable products. In fact, within circular economy systems, waste that is collected can come from either output generated from a certain company or from output generated by other companies. Hence, the return flows are very challenging to be managed by traditional IT systems.

Within this context, the circular economy moves from a traditional system based on reduce-reuse-recycle to a smart circular economy. The latter

---

[1] Pagoropoulos, A., Pigosso, D.C., & McAloone, T.C. (2017). The Emergent Role of Digital Technologies in the Circular Economy: A Review. *Procedia CIRP*, *64*, 19-24.

is defined hereby as *the circular economy system that uses a responsible digitalization approach in identifying the digital solutions and smart technologies that seek to recognize and implement the best practices to prevent the waste formation, detect efficient solutions for reducing the waste over the life cycle, search for emerging options for reusing the content obtained through circularity, apply intelligent structures for collecting, recovering, and treating materials for recycling, and use sophisticated techniques for sorting and treating circular materials to recover value and energy rather than sending them to landfill.* The adoption of smart circular economy systems allows firms to obtain information and feedback from the eco-system on circular economy related activities; therefore, smart circular economy systems enable circular knowledge, which is defined as *the justified belief that circularity is true, implies value propositions, and leads to justified actions.* This definition comes from the frequently adopted definition of knowledge by Nonaka and Takeuchi (1995) based on "justified true belief" [2], which incorporates the tripartite account of knowledge as "the truth condition, the belief condition, and the justification condition [3]. Using this triple approach to define knowledge [4], the smart circular economy can make use of digitalization to guarantee that feedstocks are available and consist of a certain quantity and quality. These elements represent a great value proposition that increases the circular economy's willingness to adopt practices and implement systems and infrastructure to appropriate such a value.

5.2. A smart circular economy through responsible digitalization

The adoption of digital technologies has been both fashionable and attractive in recent years due to the potential benefits of their use and the role they play in the digital world [5]. All transformations and technological revolutions, especially those occurring after the 1950s, have brought great prosperity, progress, and value. However, firms require further analysis to better understand such rapid and increasing trends, specifically whether

[2] Nonaka, I., o Nonaka, I., Ikujiro, N., & Takeuchi, H. (1995). *The knowledge-creating company: How Japanese companies create the dynamics of innovation* (Vol. 105). OUP USA.

[3] Neta, R., & Duncan P., (Eds.) (2009). *Arguing About Knowledge* (p. 151), London, Routledge.

[4] Bolisani, E., & Bratianu, C. (2018). The Elusive Definition of Knowledge. In *Emergent Knowledge Strategies* (pp. 1-22). Springer, Cham.

[5] Ivanov, D., Dolgui, A., & Sokolov, B. (2019). The impact of digital technology and Industry 4.0 on the ripple effect and supply chain risk analytics. *International Journal of Production Research, 57*(3), 829-846.

the transformation occurring through digital technologies provides real advantages and concrete market opportunities[6], along with social and environmental benefits. In any case, firms must perform a comprehensive analysis of the strategic behavioral changes required to properly select and use digital technologies, an accurate estimation of their economic outcomes, and a careful assessment of the implications for the entire eco-system[7]. In the past, several unintended consequences have followed industrial transformations and revolutions, including climate change and global warming, pollution, and the increasing presence of plastic in oceans, to mention a few. Therefore, the current digital transformation could have similar effects if left unchecked.

The implementation of digital technologies requires a comprehensive analysis of their adoption, including the complex regulatory, tax, auditability, risk, and compliance implications linked to global business and extended to the environmental and social spheres[8]. Restrictive legislation, reputational pressure, corruption, misleading information and products, human rights and gender violations, unknown working conditions, and security are only some of the factors firms should consider when selecting their portfolio of digital technologies. In this sense, De Giovanni (2021) coined the concept of *responsible digitalization*, which is exemplified by firms' capability of achieving their corporate social responsibility (CSR) goals by adopting digital technologies[9]. Accordingly, firms should not restrict their focus on digital technologies as merely boosters of enhancing economic performance, but, rather, they should carefully evaluate the digital technologies' implications in terms of environmental effects and social targets.

As empirically shown in De Giovanni (2021), digital technologies can harm both the social and the environmental spheres. For example, a farmer who invests in robotics can achieve positive benefits for the environment by reducing production waste and the energy used, and hence aim at reducing principles of the circular economy. However, recent estimates show that a crop-harvesting robot can replace up to 30 human workers. Therefore, robotics can generate important social "rebound effects" that any digital

---

[6] Sista, E., & De Giovanni, P. (2021). Scaling up smart city logistics projects: The case of the SMOOTh project. *Smart Cities*, *4*(4), 1337-1365.

[7] Ivanov et al. (2019). *Ibidem*.

[8] Cardinali, P.G., & De Giovanni, P. (2022). Responsible digitalization through digital technologies and green practices. *Corporate Social Responsibility and Environmental Management*. 29, 984-995.

[9] De Giovanni, P. (2021). Smart Supply Chains with vendor managed inventory, coordination, and environmental performance. *European Journal of Operational Research*, *292*(2), 515-531.

transformation process cannot disregard. Similarly, Industry 4.0 technologies can ensure true circular economy targets such as a lower scrap rate, high saturation of manufacturing equipment, low waste, and superior energy efficiency [10]. However, production systems using robotics and big data can become highly capital-intensive, which can result in overall higher energy consumption [11]. In fact, the use of big data requires data centers to consume around 200 terawatt hours annually, which is greater than the total energy consumption of some countries (e.g., Argentina, Ukraine, Thailand), half of the electricity used for transport worldwide, and around 1% of global electricity demand [12].

According to the described frameworks, digital technologies can have an uncertain and questionable effect on CSR, which requires an accurate and rigorous analysis of both the benefits and drawbacks. The adoption of artificial intelligence (AI) systems allows firms to proactively mitigate global supply chains risks and disruptions. For example, AI systems extrapolate information from the eco-system, identify possible sources of delay, and propose alternative solutions to nullify such inconveniences [13]. For example, the identification of a potential strike of a port labor force induces the AI system to suggest moving goods by plane rather than boat. Although this option ensures on-time deliveries and consumer satisfaction, it also induces important environmental damage, since transportation by plane implies higher emissions than transportation by boat. Therefore, firms achieve responsible digitalization when the adoption of digital technologies guarantees the triple bottom line (i.e., economic, social, and environmental outcomes) and, consequently, CSR goals. The numerous emerging trade-offs resulting from the circular economy impose a careful analysis of the circular economy system to implement. Therefore, when smart circular economy systems solve all possible emerging trade-offs when adopting digital technologies and solutions, responsible digitalization is achieved.

---

[10] Müller, J.M., Kiel, D., & Voigt, K.I. (2018). What drives the implementation of Industry 4.0? The role of opportunities and challenges in the context of sustainability. *Sustainability*, *10*(1), 247.

[11] Indri, M., Grau, A., & Ruderman, M. (2018). Guest editorial special section on recent trends and developments in industry 4.0 motivated robotic solutions. *IEEE Transactions on Industrial Informatics*, *14*(4), 1677-1680.

[12] Lovell, J. (2018). Big data: A big energy challenge?, Australian energy Council, October 2018.

[13] Naclerio, A.G., & De Giovanni, P. (2022). Blockchain, logistics and omnichannel for last mile and performance. The *International Journal of Logistics Management*. 33(2), 663-686.

5.3. A smart circular economy through Industry 4.0

Industry 4.0 technologies became part of modern business models, independent of the industrial application or interested sector. To create a smart circular economy, systems and infrastructure should be supported by Industry 4.0 technologies in all aspects of the waste cascade. This includes Artificial Intelligence (AI), industrial internet of things (IIoT), cloud computing (CC), big data, simulation, augmented reality, additive manufacturing, horizontal and vertical systems integration, autonomous robots, and cybersecurity.

Hereby, a focus is given on the Industry 4.0 technologies that have a direct impact on a smart circular economy system. *Artificial Intelligence* (AI) entails the smart circular economy in both phases of implementation and management. During the implementation phase, AI helps in detecting the needed architecture and design of a circular economy system by searching the most suitable 3PL to involve within the closed loop, providing analysis on the quality of returns, reducing the uncertainty of the decision-making process, positioning the collecting points, and processing facilities, disposal centers, and – more generally – the required infrastructure [14]. Instead, during the management phase, AI supports the decision-making process in optimizing logistics networks, taking external information (e.g., temperature) to minimize the use of resources in circular systems, capturing uncertain behavior to adjust resource usage (e.g., increasing number of positive COVID cases will result in a waste increase in a certain territory) [15]. Therefore, using a network of sensors, cameras and radar devices connected to AI, the future of the circular economy can benefit from AI through autonomous smart circular systems.

Internet of Things (IoT) and Industrial Internet of Things (IIoT) rely on the key roots of the circular economy based on the maximum utilization of assets. In fact, circularity requires the existence of a connection between the circular system and those assets, to check and obtain information about various parameters and features over the life cycle.

IoT enables firms and stakeholders to obtain batches of such information by either using sensors that are directly applied on the product or injected in the eco-system, or making use of intelligent devices spread over

[14] Wilson, M., Paschen, J., & Pitt, L. (2021). The circular economy meets artificial intelligence (AI): Understanding the opportunities of AI for Reverse Logistics. *Management of Environmental Quality: An International Journal.* 33(1), 9-25

[15] Trabucco, M. & De Giovanni, P. (2021). Achieving Resilience and Business Sustainability during Covid-19: The role of Lean Supply Chain Practices and Digitalization. *Sustainability,* 13(22), 1-16.

the eco-system to recognize the product and obtain information on it. Examples of information to be collected are asset locations, conditions, quality, users, and performance. The collected information is then transferred to a *Cloud*, in which *Big Data* makes use of the information to improve the decision-making process and pursue the best sustainable strategy according to the waste cascade level the return can be associated with. These implications encourage the premise of thinking about the circular economy as a smart system, in which physical goods become smart objects and give rise to new paradigms such as smart city, smart factory, preventive maintenance, and smart home. In fact, the general business and industrial paradigms are engineered using the slogan "*anytime, anywhere, and anyone connected*", whose goal is to ensure a connection between devices with storage, production, and exchange of information and data in real time [16].

Among the various paradigms, *IIoT* is emerging as a robust technology through which sensors belonging to different smart objects can interact, providing integrated knowledge on assets and connecting them to optimize the circular system as a whole [17]. Malik et al. (2021) show various applications of IIoT, whose potential can be enabled by investing in connecting technologies like wifi, mobile, wimax, and bluetooth. Hereby, they also show how IIoT is successfully applied to the whole life cycle, from product design to recycling activity [18].

3D printing, also called additive manufacturing, is a technology through which objects can be created from CAD systems or digital 3D models by adding layers of materials that are deposited, joined, and solidified until the final product is obtained. 3D printing allows firms to reduce at a minimum the production scale [19] and better align the production to the market demand [20]. According to Garmulewicz et al. (2018), 3D printing feedstock can be metals and biomass, although plastics are the most common materi-

---

[16] Hassan, R., Qamar, F., Hasan, M.K., Aman, A.H.M., & Ahmed, A.S. (2020). Internet of Things and Its Applications: A Comprehensive Survey. *Symmetry, 12*(10), 1674.

[17] De Giovanni, P. (2021). Digital Supply Chain Through IoT, Design Quality, and Circular Economy. In *Dynamic Quality Models and Games in Digital Supply Chains.* (pp. 57-89). Springer, Cham.

[18] Malik, P.K., Sharma, R., Singh, R., Gehlot, A., Satapathy, S.C., Alnumay, W.S., & Nayak, J. (2021). Industrial Internet of Things and Its Applications in Industry 4.0: State of the Art. *Computer Communications, 166*, 125-139.

[19] Cotteleer, M.J. (2014), 3D Opportunity for Production. *Deloitte Review, 15*, 146-161.

[20] Ben-Ner, A., & Siemsen, E. (2017). Decentralization and Localization of Production: The Organizational and Economic Consequences of Additive Manufacturing (3D printing). *California Management Review, 59*(2), 5-23.

als applied through this technology[21]. From a circular economy point of view, plastics are fully recyclable, and their low-value density implies high costs for transportation and management. Locating 3D printing facilities close to the feedstock of plastics surely represents an effective solution to enable the circular economy.

Indeed, more digital technologies can be implemented to achieve smart circular economy systems, whose evaluation should also consider both the barriers and the challenges. Reuter (2016) identified barriers to the circular economy to become smart through digitalization, with a particular focus on metals[22]. One of most important barriers is the full analysis of product recycling, which identifies the full nonlinear effects of the recovery and loss of all materials, to screen opportunities and avoid contamination. Digital tools must be used in an integrated way to achieve the full potential of digitalization by identifying portfolios of digital technologies to implement. Firms should undertake real-time big-data approaches to calibrate production, recycling, and circular economy system models that create a basis to optimize the processing chain (e.g., use of digital twin).

5.4. A smart circular economy through reverse omnichannel strategies

Although the field of the circular economy has primarily focused on the networks to implement in order to make it successful, atypical collection structures are emerging today, and they consider omnichannel options. In its original form, omnichannel plays a strategic role in enabling e-commerce and ensuring seamless purchasing experiences for consumers[23]. Therefore, firms' attitudes to integrate offline and online channels to provide a seamless customer experience finds its roots in continuous technological development[24], rapid changes related to consumer purchasing habits[25], and the

---

[21] Garmulewicz, A., Holweg, M., Veldhuis, H., & Yang, A. (2018). Disruptive Technology as an Enabler of the Circular Economy: What Potential Does 3D Printing Hold? *California Management Review*, *60*(3), 112-132.

[22] Reuter, M.A. (2016). Digitalizing the Circular Economy. *Metallurgical and Materials Transactions B*, *47*(6), 3194-3220.

[23] Levy, M., Weitz, B., & Grewal, D. (2013). Retailing Management. New York: McGraw-Hill Education.

[24] Brynjolfsson, E., Hu, Y.J., & Rahman, M.S. (2013). Competing in the Age of Omnichannel Retailing. *MIT Sloan Management Review*, 1-7.

[25] Genc, T.S., & De Giovanni, P. (2021). Dynamic pricing and green investments under conscious, emotional, and rational consumers. *Cleaner and Responsible Consumption*, *2*, 100007.

benefits that omnichannel offers in terms of sales growth, brand loyalty, and customer satisfaction[26]. The literature has deeply detailed the possible advantages and potential applications of omnichannel and has also documented the phenomenon through various case studies (e.g., Tesco and Macy's). However, omnichannel also offers unimaginable opportunities when applied to circular economy systems[27]. In fact, along with its traditional forward functions, omnichannel is suitable in engaging consumers in reverse activities, including returning products to retail stores, shipping them back to manufacturers' or retailers' warehouses, and returning them to the manufacturer's factory or a locker[28]. De Giovanni (2022) defines reverse omnichannel as firms' capability of offering and integrating various collection options for consumers with the purpose of gaining economic value through atypical collection opportunities[29].

Several business cases reinforce the motivation for firms to evaluate the implementation of reverse omnichannel. A research study conducted by Lau et al. (2015) demonstrates that 72% of consumers who make purchases online return such products in a physical store, thereby activating reverse omnichannel options[30]. Within a theoretical framework, Jin et al. (2020) study how the configuration buy-online-return-offline offers important opportunities to create competitive advantages[31]. Hence, reverse logistics systems can integrate the traditional forward and reverse flows over all existing channels, and the reverse omnichannel solution as well, through which consumers have different options for returning their products, collectors optimize the logistics path according to the locations defined in the omnichannel strategy, and the return process can exhibit a high degree of uncertainty.

---

[26] Naclerio, A G. and De Giovanni, P. (2022). *Ibidem*.

[27] Xu, X., & Jackson, J.E. (2019). Investigating the influential factors of return channel loyalty in omnichannel retailing. *International Journal of Production Economics, 216*, 118-132.

[28] Bell, D.R., Gallino, S., & Moreno, A. (2014). How to win in an omnichannel world. *MIT Sloan Management Review, 56*(1), 45-51.

[29] De Giovanni, P. (2022). Leveraging the Circular Economy with Closed-loop Supply Chain and Reverse Omnichannel using Blockchain Technology and Incentives. *International Journal of Operations and Production Management,* 42(7), 959-994.

[30] Lau, A., Chi, J., Gong, F., Li, L., & Liao, N. (2015). China's iConsumer 2015: A growing appetite for choice and change. McKinsey & Company, http://www. mckinseychina. com/chinasiconsumer-2015-a-growing-appetite-for-change/.

[31] Jin, D., Caliskan-Demirag, O., Chen, F.Y., & Huang, M. (2020). Omnichannel retailers' return policy strategies in the presence of competition. *International Journal of Production Economics, 225*, 107595.

A reverse omnichannel strategy is then a set of options given to consumers to finalize the return process in atypical ways [32]. It can be seen as information surrounding the return points, stock-keeping points, and product reverse flows that are retrievable, traceable, and changeable over all channels. The literature and the business models are quite rich in terms of the analysis of omnichannel solutions linked to forward goods, in which process consumers can purchase either online or offline and receive the delivery at home (e.g., home delivery), at a certain location (e.g., lockers), or at a company location (e.g., delivery to a store). The omnichannel solutions that firms guarantee most likely lack the presence of a reverse omnichannel strategy that, within the forward omnichannel strategies, consists of several combinations between the activation of the return process and the physical collection of products. Therefore, reverse omnichannel strategies require end users to have the chance to return their goods by initiating the return process, either online (e.g., through an app) or offline (e.g., visiting the seller), and finalizing the return process, either by having collectors visit their home (e.g., home collection), having them go to a certain location (e.g., return to a collecting location), or meeting at a company location (e.g., return to the seller's location). These options offer new ways to manage and return content and reinforce the potential of circular economy systems.

5.5. A smart circular economy through smart cities

According to EIP (2013), smart cities should be regarded as systems of people interacting with and using flows of energy, materials, services and financing to catalyze sustainable economic development, resilience, and high quality of life; these flows and interactions become smart through the strategic use of information and communication infrastructure and services in a process of transparent urban planning and management that is responsive to the social and economic needs of society [33].

Within this framework, the smart circular economy can help to implement digital systems to make smart cities more efficient. The implementation of circular systems in modern society comes with several important barriers, among which are technological, regulatory, financial, managerial, performance-indicator, consumer, and social barriers [34]. However, a lack

---

[32] De Giovanni, P. (2022). *Ibidem*.

[33] EIP on Smart Cities and Communities - Strategic and Implementation Plan, 2013.

[34] Darla, G., Galvão, A., De Nadae, J., Honorato, D., Stief, P., Dantan, J., & Siadat, A. (2018). *Circular Economy: Overview of Barriers*. Procedia CIRP, *73*, 79-85. doi: 10.1016/j.procir.2018.04.011.

information and the absence of intelligent systems to create and diffuse knowledge are the major constraints that smart cities face.

Interestingly, smart cities combine advanced wireless sensors, information, and communication technology to help effectively manage a city's assets[35]. Wireless sensors are applicable in a variety of options and situations to detect, calculate, measure, and monitor the eco-system. Hence, the sensors allow the connection between a smart city and a smart circular economy system. The sensors can transmit data on various feedstock cumulated from the territory and offer a genuine opportunity to proactively implement circular practices. Nowadays, sensors are relatively cheap and require negligible power and maintenance costs, favoring the digitalization of all physical assets. One interesting application of smart devices over smart cities is the smart bin. People and users who have to get rid of garbage can use an app to check the available bins with some empty space across a city. The app shows the availability according to the type of waste to dispose of, thus enabling a smart circular economy. The intelligent bins not only connect and drive users to proper waste management, but also inform the collectors about the existence of bins to be emptied, capacity utilization, and the type of waste to collect. Therefore, the intelligent bins allow collectors to optimize reverse logistics activities by collecting and analyzing the data received from the bins' sensors[36]. The use of smart bins implies an incremental innovation in the city and provides advantages in terms of the following: Understanding the production of waste in a city, improving the environment in a city, providing citizens with more efficient waste management, evaluating the bin infrastructure in the city in terms of density, efficiency and cost, optimizing waste bin capacity, location, and type, optimizing waste collection frequencies, reducing costs, being able to collect waste on demand, reflecting the actual need, relieving traffic congestion in a city related to regular waste collection routes, providing citizens with a free mobile app enabling them to find the nearest available empty bin, and providing directions and single-click notification to the operators[37].

Unlike smart bins, smart cities can be organized with radical innovation investments through smart circular economy projects. Some companies (e.g., Envac) propose smart circular economy solutions for cities by implementing a collection system based on vacuum technology. People, firms,

---

[35] Li, X., Bao, J., Sun, J., & Wang, J. (2021). Development of Circular Economy in Smart Cities Based on FPGA and Wireless Sensors. *Microprocessors and Microsystems, 80*, 103600.

[36] Grattard G., & OUTSMART Consortium (2013), *OUTSMART Annual Report 2013*, available at: http://www.fi-ppp-outsmart.eu/.

[37] https://sensoneo.com/smart-waste-management-solution-for-cities/.

and stakeholders do not leave and/or collect garbage and waste in traditional modes (e.g., putting it inside bins or leaving it outside the home door) but, rather, put the garbage inside some collection points that are connected to long pipelines in which a vacuum system brings the garbage underground. Hereby, the whole waste management system is organized, and circular economy principles, as described in the waste cascade, can be applied. This system allows cities to remove the traditional operations linked to waste management, such as waste collection, transportation, and sorting. The recycling activities become smart, since the circular economy principles are applied at the upstream of a circular economy chain. This avoids that cities face issues in terms of open waste containers, overflowing waste bins, and traffic jams and pollution caused by waste collection vehicles[38]. Furthermore, the sealed system removes foul smells, can be easily placed close to residential buildings, and completely remedies littering issues. Other positive side effects result from this solution: Less noise due to diminished waste collection traffic, lower emissions and pollution, and better usage of the public space.

One interesting feature of smart cities pertains to the circular economy of energy systems. Smart cities are in fact supposed to meet a significant portion of total energy requirements on their own. Therefore, circular economy systems should be activated to manage waste, and conserve and reuse water, energy, and resources. Residents may contribute to the production of electrical power (e.g., through solar panels or small biomass plant systems) and clean water (through recycling and purifying systems). This will lead to a lower consumption of natural resources like gas and methane. Residents can use various forms of resource-to-grid systems to contribute to circularity, taking the form of energy-to-grid or water-to-grid. These new frameworks require the vital support of digital technologies, which should connect residents' circular economy behavior to the entire city's infrastructure, which is composed of energy systems, bio-systems, local resource management, and waste collection and treatment systems. All of these infrastructures require the use of digital technologies to guarantee circular systems' proper functioning.

---

[38] Check Envac's webpage for a full description of the smart waste management solutions proposed for smart cities https://www.envacgroup.com/what-we-do/.

Part II

Chapter 1
CIRCULAR GREEN DISTRICTS

Pierroberto Folgiero

ABSTRACT: *This chapter focuses on the study of a practical case: the Green Circular District. The model is a technological platform of green chemistry technologies, such as those dedicated to the mechanical and chemical recycling of waste for the production of building blocks, including methanol, ethanol, and hydrogen. The analysis focused on the technological and economic structure of the model, identifying future prospects for the green circular district as an enabler of environmental transition.*

1.1. Defining Green Circular Districts

The transition from a linear economy to a circular economy is a pressing matter dictated by the guidelines of the European Commission and the urge to reduce the supply of virgin raw materials while increasing waste recovery. This applies to all waste, but in particular to plastic waste, for which recycling efficiency still lags behind the targets set by Europe, with incorrect management severely impacting the environment and damaging natural resources and fauna. At the same time, the need to contain climate change caused by global warming through a reduction in the amount of CO_2 released into the atmosphere urges us to act rapidly under the European guidelines.

The European Union (EU) seeks to accelerate the transition toward a regenerative growth model by reducing its consumption footprint and doubling the rate of circular materials used over the next decade [1]. In line with the objectives outlined in its industrial strategy, the EU seeks to promote circularity in industrial processes, facilitating industrial symbiosis and the use of green technologies. This type of green industrial infrastructure

[1] EC (2020). New Circular Economy Action Plan.

throughout the ecological transition toward the decarbonization of the economy in terms of circularity is essential to achieve the EU's objectives. The new EU Waste Directive strengthens the policy and aims to close the landfills on European soil on a mandatory and progressive basis and minimize the use of incineration compared to recycling and recovery.

Europe has a worldwide leadership position in plastic recycling and in circular solutions. However, three major problems remain largely unsolved:

- Market launching of high-quality recycled polymers that could replace virgin plastics in high-end applications and increase the effective recycling rate.
- The problem of waste plastics, which are still primarily incinerated or sent to landfills.
- The problem of refuse-derived fuel (RDF) and waste dry fraction that need to be recovered.

Therefore, the priorities concern the increase in the mechanical high-quality recycling rate and the development of solutions for non-mechanically recyclable fractions to reach more ambitious objectives using new technologies and adequate plant infrastructures.

Decarbonization of the economy through circularity can start with the green adaptation of existing industrial plants currently based on fossil feedstocks and the development of new process solutions to use biological or circular origin feedstock (derived from circular economy processes), capable of making low-carbon products. Such solutions, which are technically mature and which can be industrially realized, should become part of an industrial recovery and green transition plan.

Process solutions for the production of circular chemicals from currently non-recyclable waste fractions (therefore representing an economic, social, and environmental cost) allow for the replacement of fossil sources in industrial processes (such as natural gas or hydrogen produced from methane) with feedstocks having a lower carbon footprint than those feedstocks from fossil origin. Furthermore, such solutions allow for the reduction of both industrial CO_2 emissions and the amount of waste to be either incinerated or taken to landfills.

The concept of a Green Circular District has been developed by NextChem – Maire Tecnimont's energy transition company – and is a model that facilitates the production of recycled polymers, chemicals, hydrogen, and fuels with low carbon content by recycling plastic and recovering non-recyclable waste.

The Green Circular District is a "circular" technological and industrial platform (Figure 1) that integrates both plastic recycling for the production of new, low-carbon-impact chemicals and the chemical recycling of plastic and dry waste, which cannot otherwise be recovered, for the production of chemicals and circular fuels. These products have a smaller carbon footprint than those derived from fossil-based sources and can be used for sustainable mobility and industrial production. The model also incorporates the production of green hydrogen from renewable energy via electrolysis into a technological platform.

The model of the Green Circular District enables the production of new materials and new substances with a smaller environmental impact than those manufactured from virgin raw materials, while also facilitating resource savings by recovering those resources already in circulation. The Green Circular District can become the driving force for the shift from a linear economy (manufacture-consume-dispose) to a circular one (manufacture-consume-recycle-remanufacture) using materials and substances derived from recycling and designing products to make them last longer and increase their circularity. Materials and substances derived from recycling can then be used again in the production of goods, and in the energy and chemical industries, improving overall environmental impacts. In addition to environmental benefits and those tied to reducing dependence on foreign imports by nationally producing vital chemicals for industry (of which Italy is currently a net importer), the Green Circular District Model can revitalize local economies, creating new ancillary trade and supply chains downstream.

Figure 1. The Circular District Model.

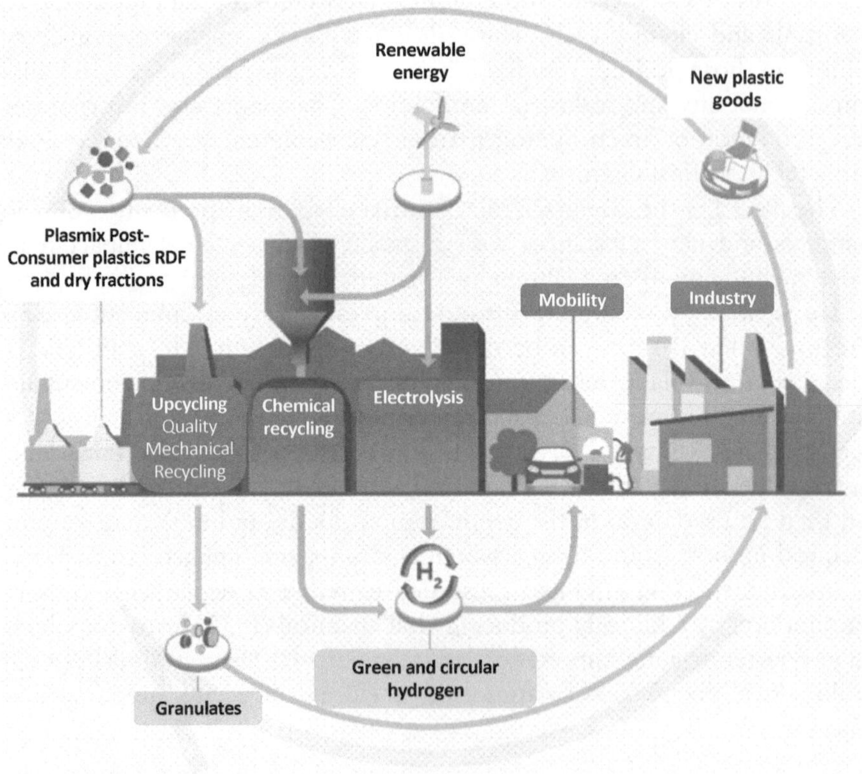

1.2. Green Circular Districts as enablers of energy transition

Green chemistry and the circular economy have in recent decades been considered two different and parallel streams, the first of which is aimed at contributing to decarbonization through the use of renewable sources and biogenic feedstocks, and the second of which is aimed at reducing the consumption of natural resources and raw materials and improving the capability of reuse of existing resources and materials through eco-design, recycling and symbiosis.

These trends are now evolving into a third one (Figure 2), in which green chemistry and the circular economy are combined to create decarbonized circular molecules from green electrons and waste, with an approach that considers economic sustainability and the value of the obtained products.

Figure 2. The new paradigm of the green circular economy.

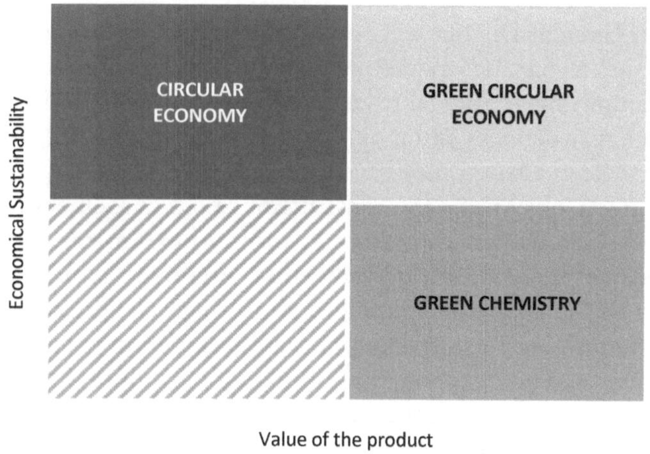

The outcomes of a Green Circular District are as follows:

- Recycled polymers, which are used to manufacture new plastic objects (such as, for example, automotive components), that become waste to be recycled anew once they reach the end-of-use stage.
- Circular Gas™, which can be used to produce hydrogen, methanol, ethanol, ammonia, and many derivatives that are vital to the production of fuels and any kind of object.
- Green hydrogen through an electrolysis process that starts with water and renewable energy sources, like the sun and the wind. Hydrogen can be used as a fuel in industry and transportation.

Green Circular Districts can yield significant reductions in industrial emissions. Many fossil resources can be saved by replacing virgin plastics with recycled plastics, by producing low carbon chemicals, and by creating fuels that contribute to the decarbonization of the transport and industrial sectors. These benefits entail a reduction in CO_2 emissions that would otherwise be produced if that waste were disposed of through incineration or placement in landfills. The model introduces a paradigm shift that overturns the concept of waste as a problem to get rid of and replaces the chemistry of coal and oil with chemistry based on the recovery of resources which would otherwise be lost.

The Green Circular District seeks to ensure that the already low CO_2 emissions generated by recycling plants are vastly compensated by the CO_2 savings from both avoiding waste incineration and landfill disposal, as well as the manufacture of "circular" products instead of fossil-based ones. Furthermore, with the use of renewable energy to power the plant and the integration of electrolysis in the technological model, carbon neutrality over the whole system can definitely be achieved.

The Green Circular District will be fully digitalized, ensuring preventive analysis of maintenance and operational data, maximizing annual operating hours, and minimizing accidental risks. In addition, the use of digitalization enables remote management and monitoring of facilities.

A Circular Green District may have a considerable social impact by creating several green jobs during the construction and management phases. A Circular Green District can contribute to private investments to promote economic recovery in strategic green sectors, preserve employment over supply chains and in fragile geographic areas through reskilling, and create new jobs, including for young people, through training in specialized professional resources. The dissemination of know-how will favor the uptake of these solutions in other industrial sectors and companies; consequently, new down-stream supply chains can be created, as well as new local momentum toward positive social and economic development.

Considering the environmental benefits (reduction of waste sent to landfill or incinerated, reduction of CO_2 emissions), the social benefits (more jobs, reskilling), and the economic benefits (new ancillary trade and supply-chains downstream), the Circular Green District is a winning strategy in terms of ecological transition. Above all, it can be an opportunity for industries with many obsolete plants to be converted into green ones.[2] Existing jobs can be protected, and new green jobs can be created in this restoration process, supporting sustainable, low-emission economic development.

1.3. Technology adoption in Green Circular Districts

The district can be considered a "local" model, because – having been conceived for the green redevelopment of traditional industrial sites without further land use – it would become a "concentrated" green chemistry hub for the recycling and recovery of plastic waste and the production of circular chemical products (Figure 2). Converted traditional refineries provide the perfect location to house the District. Ideally, these would include an area for incoming waste (being, in many cases, already equipped with railway tracks), an upcycling facility for recyclable plastic waste, and an adjacent waste to chemicals plant for the recovery of non-recyclable plastic and non-recyclable waste. In fact, their proximity would allow residues from the upcycling process to still be recovered in the second plant. Further-

[2] ISPRA (2021). Sites of National Interest.

more, other areas would be needed, such as for an electrolyzer for the production of green hydrogen from renewable energy plants located nearby, and an area to store the output of circular products, with suitable storage tanks.

Figure 3. The technological steps of a Green Circular District.

1) Our Green Circular District modelenables the production of recycled polymers, chemicals, hydrogen, and low carbon-content fuels by recycling plastic and recovering non-recyclable waste.

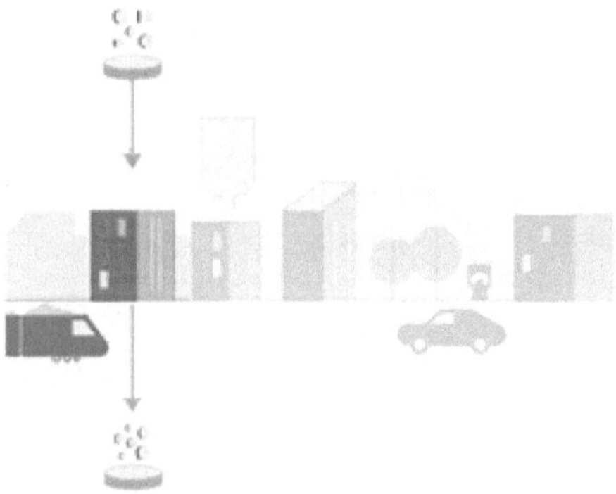

2) Some plastic waste can be recycled mechanically thank to our MyReplast™ upcycling tecnology, resulting in new high-quality recycled polymers.

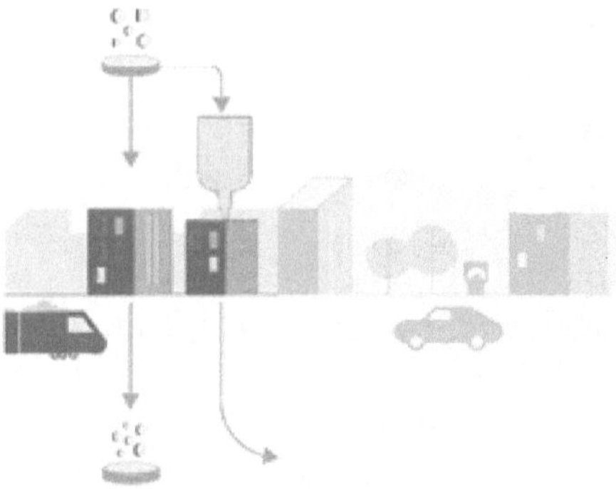

3) Non-recyclable plastic and non-recyclable waste can be chemically converted to recover the carbon and hydrogen contained within it, through a process called partial oxidation. This does not involve combustion and creates a Circular Gas™ that is used to produce chemicals and green fuels, such as circular hydrogen

continued

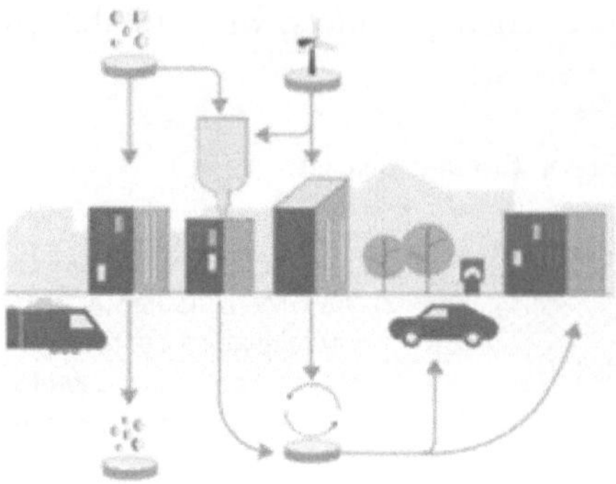

4) The Green Circular District can also produce green hydrogen through an eletrolysis process that starts whit water and renewable energy sources. Hydrogen can be used as a fuel for civil and industrial purposes, and will increasingly be seen as the fuel of the future.

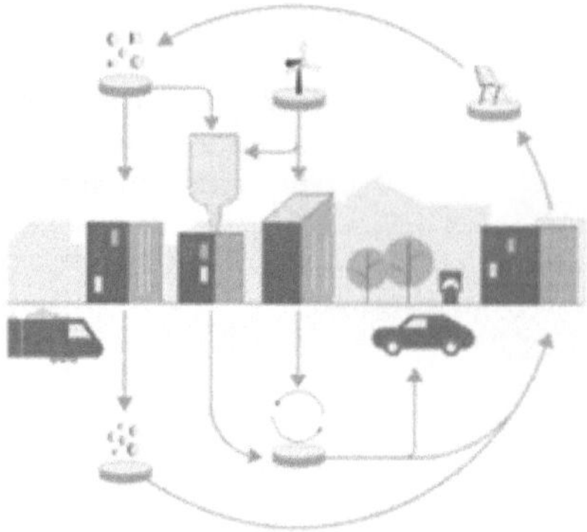

5) The process does not end there. Recycled polymers are used to manufacture new plastic object (such as, for example, automotive components) that, once their use-life cycle has ended, will once again become waste than can be recycled anew.

The model developed by NextChem has a structure designed to serve the waste hierarchy (Figure 3): High-quality mechanical recycling (upcycling) of plastic waste, chemical recycling of residual plastic and dry waste. Furthermore, with the addition of an electrolyzer, it is possible to enable the production of green hydrogen by electrolysis.

Upcycling is a technology employed to mechanically recycle post-consumer plastic waste, and to obtain, after chemical treatment, recycled high added value polymer. In the upcycling process, the selection is based on polymers and colors, followed by a volumetric reduction to obtain flakes. In the subsequent chemical treatment, the flakes are extruded together with additives to obtain granulates. The products obtained through upcycling have chemical and physical characteristics like virgin plastic. Upcycling efficiency is remarkably high (95%), and 5% of waste can still be recovered through the waste to chemicals technology.

Waste to chemicals uses non-recyclable waste, like that generated from packaging sorting, and refuse-derived fuel, as well as the dry fraction of undifferentiated waste. Chemical recycling (waste to chemicals) is a chemical conversion process involving non-mechanically recyclable waste (therefore not competing with mechanical recycling) that produces a synthesis gas used to produce compounds such as hydrogen, methanol, and circular ethanol.

Figure 4. Waste Management Hierarchy.

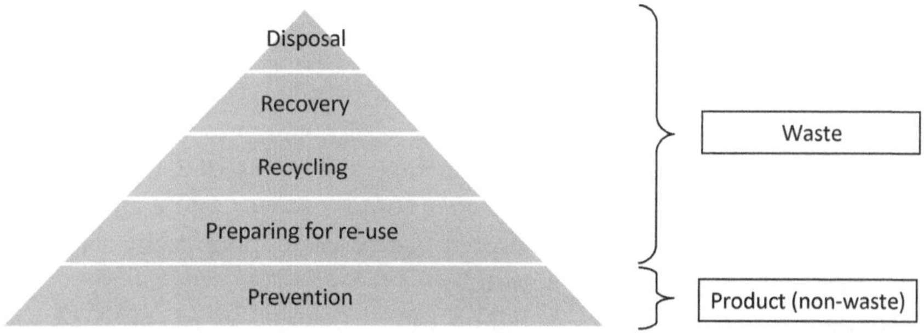

Electrolysis is the third potential component of a Circular Green District. It is a technology used to make green hydrogen from water and renewable energy sources. Adding a renewable electrolyzer to produce hydrogen will further lower the carbon footprint of the waste to chemicals process. Renewable hydrogen, in addition to that obtained through the waste to chemicals process, helps to curb CO_2 emissions. Without electrolysis, waste to chemicals CO_2 would add to emissions, albeit to a lesser extent. Therefore, renewable hydrogen increases the conversion ratio, enabling greater circular product output and improving the carbon neutrality of the plant.

Together, these three technologies constitute the basis for a Green Circular District, obtaining high added value recycled polymers through upcycling.

In the future, the district could also be compatible with other chemical recycling technologies, such as pyrolysis and the depolymerization of selected fractions of plastic waste, including PET and polyester textile waste, or the production of biofuels from waste vegetable oils, fats, or waste biomass.

1.4. Identification of secure feedstocks and final product markets

1.4.1. Potential feedstocks of a Green Circular District

Waste to chemicals does not compete with mechanical recycling, but it does integrate and enhance the former. Waste that cannot be mechanically recycled can be treated by waste to chemicals / fuels recycling technology. This means that plastic packaging waste coming from urban waste sorting amounting to about 40% of the total urban sorted waste and refuse-derived fuel (RDF), a fraction of undifferentiated urban waste that, after a selection process, reaches lower moisture content and a higher calorific value.

Upcycling and waste to chemicals are innovative, valid and indispensable solutions in the future carbon-neutral world, which has no place for incinerators (an incinerator emits on average 1.35 tons of CO_2 per ton of waste). Each "green circular district" could recover on average about 230,000 tons of recyclable and non-recyclable waste, potentially also recovering waste already placed in landfills.

In Italy, approximately 6.3 million tons[3] of waste were disposed of in landfills in 2019. According to an estimate, building 10 circular districts in Italy, one-third of the waste currently sent to landfills could be recycled. Ten districts could absorb 2.6 million tons/year of waste, which constitutes 8.81% of the total waste produced in 2019 in Italy. At the European level, 10 districts would yield a 1% reduction in waste produced in Europe and a potential 4.5% reduction in waste sent to landfills.

This model has been developed to strive for "zero waste", meaning that the waste output of recycling processes is constantly decreasing and is generally never higher than 5% of the material input. Furthermore, the model is designed to manage waste by ideally aiming for a "locally-sourced" approach, minimizing waste transport costs (waste is currently often disposed of in places located far from where it was created) and the environmental impact (in terms of pollution and climate-altering emissions) derived from transportation.

1.4.2 Final product markets

The final products of a Green Circular District may be as follows:

- Recycled polymers (PE and PP)

[3] ISPRA (2020). Urban Waste Report.

- Circular Gas
- Circular ethanol
- Circular methanol
- Circular hydrogen
- Green hydrogen.

Recycled polymers

Plastics are among the most popular materials in use in everyday life. In 2019, global plastics production reached 370 million tons. To date, most plastics are produced on a fossil basis, and only 21.3% of the world's production is recycled[4]. Through upcycling technology, it is possible to mechanically recycle post-consumer plastics and to obtain high added value recycled polymers with the chemical and physical properties of virgin plastics, thanks to the chemical extrusion of plastic flakes mixed with special additives.

Polyethylene (PE) is a plastic polymer widely used in the packaging, transport, and construction industries due to its resistance to wear. There are two variants of PE, one high density (HDPE, or high density polyethylene) and one low density (LDPE, or low density polyethylene). Once recycled, it is available in the form of granules, which are characterized by a medium viscosity and a very low mineral charge suitable for the molding of saucers and jars. Through the upcycling technology, it is possible to also produce PE in flakes, characterized by high/medium viscosity and suitable for the manufacture of industrial drums, jerry cans, and pipes.

Polypropylene (PP) is a versatile plastic material used in packaging, construction, and automotive components. In recycled form, PP has strong impact strength and is suitable for injection-molding large items with high wall thickness, including packaging, household items, construction tools, electrical appliances, and automotive components.

Recycled **polyolefins** (PO) offer a cost-effective opportunity to add recycled polyolefin content to compounds or molded products, maintaining strong processability and constant performance. Recycled PO products are suitable for the injection molding of various items, such as crates, bins, and pallets.

Circular gas

Waste, such as RDF, municipal solid waste, and waste plastics, once properly converted into **Circular Gas™**, can be used in several fields. Thanks to its

---

[4] Tiseo, I. (2020). Global waste generation-statistics & facts. Available at: https://www.statista.com/topics/4983/waste-generation-worldwide/#dossierKeyfigures.

reducing qualities, it can be used in hard-to-abate production processes, such as the steel industry, as a cheaper and low carbon replacement of synthesis gas derived from methane or coal derivatives (such as carbon dust). Circular Gas can also be used as a basis for the production of circular hydrogen, methanol, ethanol, and a variety of other chemical compounds essential for the industry. These products can be used in a multitude of fields: Both as chemicals in many industries (e.g., the furniture industry and health care products) and as low-carbon fuels, and also as feedstock for the synthesis of a wide range of chemicals.

Circular methanol

Methanol is a well-known building block in the chemical industry. In 2019, global production of methanol stood at 98.3 Mt. The largest global producer and consumer of methanol is China (Figure 5), which is attributed more than half of global demand, followed by Asia, Europe, and North and South America[5]. Almost 100% of methanol production is considered high carbon intensity: 65% is based on natural gas reformation (grey methanol), while the rest (35%) is largely based on coal gasification (brown methanol)[6].

According to IRENA forecasts, world production of methanol could grow to 500 Mt per year by 2050, with an annual release of emissions equal to 1.5 Gt of CO_2 into the atmosphere. More than 60% of global production is used for the synthesis of chemical substances such as formaldehyde, acetic acid, methyl methacrylate, and ethylene and propylene. Methanol is also used as a solvent, antifreeze, windscreen washer fluid, and for denitrification in wastewater treatment plants. Since the mid-2000s, the use of methanol to produce methyl-t-butyl ether (MTBE) and dimethyl ether (DME) has increased, accounting for 31% of global demand.

---

[5] Irena and Methanol Institute (2021). Innovation Outlook: Renewable Methanol, International Renewable Energy Agency, Abu Dhabi.

[6] Dolan, G.A. (2020). "Methanol: Emerging global energy markets," Methanol Institute, presentation for 16th Annual State of the Energy Industry Forum, Washington, DC, 23 January.

Figure 5. Our elaboration based on data from MMSA (2022).

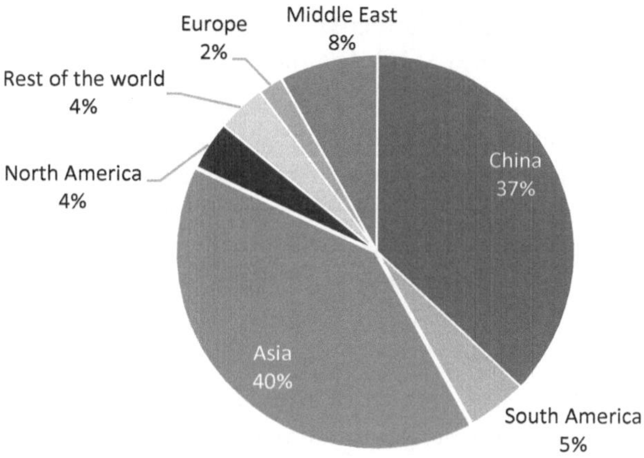

The increase of marine transport, estimated to be at approximately 3.4% to the year for the period spanning from 2019-2024, and the consequent increase of emissions are influencing the field toward more sustainable choices in terms of fuels. Given its similar physical properties to conventional marine fuels, low CO_2 and NO_X emissions and zero SO_X and PM emissions, and that it is possible to burn it in diesel engines with various combustion strategies, methanol is positioned as an alternative solution to LNG in maritime transport[7].

Circular ethanol

Ethanol is the most widely used liquid biofuel in the world. One of its uses is in fact being mixed with gasoline up to 10% for the production of E10, but it is also available in E85, where the amount of ethanol is 85%. Ethanol production is primarily located in the United States and Brazil, holding 53% and 31% of world production capacity, respectively[8]. Ethanol produced in America is mainly derived from corn, while in Brazil it is primarily derived from sugar cane[9]. Although COVID-19 significantly affected global ethanol production in 2020, which dropped to 26 billion gallons in the

[7] Zincir, B., & Deniz, C. (2021). Methanol as a fuel for marine diesel engines. In *Alcohol as an Alternative Fuel for Internal Combustion Engines* (pp. 45-85). Springer, Singapore.

[8] Renewable Fuels Association. (2021). Essential Energy, 2021 Ethanol Industry Outlook. Renewable Fuel Organization. Available at: https://d35t1syewk4d42.cloudfront.net/file/1007/RFA_Outlook_2021_fin_low.pdf.

[9] Dutta, A. (2020). Are global ethanol markets a 'one great pool'? *Biomass and Bioenergy*, *132*, 105436.

same year, the industry's largest players have not changed.

Ethanol is also used in healthcare. A study published by the WHO showed the possibility of achieving effective inactivation of bacteria by disinfectants composed of 70% ethanol [10]. Ethanol is also used as an antidote in cases of intoxication by methanol or ethylene glycol, reducing the production of toxic metabolites of methanol and ethylene glycol [11]. Another interesting use of ethanol is in the production of shellac, used for the treatment of wood furniture for the improvement of its biological resistance, but also as a promising material for new drug or pesticide delivery systems.

Circular hydrogen

Hydrogen is emerging as a key element in energy transition. Hydrogen, in fact, is at the center of the challenges related to global warming, and its characteristics render it a fundamental energy carrier. In fact, it proves usable as both a fuel and a raw chemical material in many industrial processes, and it is storable and transportable over long distances. Hydrogen is an important building block in the chemical industry in the synthesis of ammonia and methanol, and in the production of fertilizers. It is also used in refineries in direct iron reduction processes for steel production.

In 2020, the global demand for hydrogen reached 90 Mt, which was met almost entirely by a production involving the reforming of natural gas, coal gasification and lignite, associated with a release of 900 Mt of climate-altering emissions into the atmosphere (IEA, 2021). China is the largest user and producer of hydrogen in the world, with an annual consumption of over 24 Mt. The high transport costs of hydrogen directly affect international trade, which is still limited. In fact, 85% of the hydrogen gas produced is consumed on site in a plant rather than being bought and sold on the wider market [12].

Through the Green Circular District, it will be possible to produce products such as synthetic gas, methanol, ethanol, and low carbon hydrogen locally, reducing imports and meeting energy demand thanks to products obtained from the circular economy.

---

[10] World Health Organization (WHO) (2019), Water, sanitation, hygiene, and waste management for SARS-CoV-2, the virus that causes COVID-19: Interim guidance.29 July 2020 (No WHO/2019-nCOV/IPC_WASH/2020.4). World Health Organization.

[11] Le Dare, B., & Gicquel, T. (2019). Therapeutic applications of ethanol: A review. *Journal of Pharmacy & Pharmaceutical Sciences*, 22, 525-535.

[12] Irena (2022). Geopolitics of the Energy Transformation: The Hydrogen Factor, International Renewable Energy Agency, Abu Dhabi.

1.5. The economic feasibility of a Green Circular District

In order to prepare the industrial system for the reduction of risks and economic losses due to climate change, and to face their impact on many sectors, it is necessary to rebuild the industrial system quickly, but also in a long-lasting manner. Long-term sustainable investments in green and innovative technologies will attract more and more private capital, because they are the key to future-resilient economies – rather than from investments that aim to maintain the status quo. Innovation is the lever of economic growth. Innovation today is directed toward the development of technologies that are able to create long-lasting value that meets the requirements of circular, decarbonized, sustainable development. COVID-19 has made it clear how important industrial autonomy is for a country, and that national economies must become resilient to crises and shocks. Thanks to green chemistry, it is possible to produce a basket of locally produced goods, ensuring the self-sufficiency of the country itself in terms of raw materials, products, and energy. Green chemistry can help to create molecules that, until today, were thought to be produced only with traditional chemistry and based on fossil sources. Examples of green chemistry are biochemistry, electrochemistry, and waste chemistry. Industries still have a long way to go in terms of innovating sectors and scaling up technologies. Although the transition from fossil to renewable energy production is taking place more and more rapidly, it will be a gradual process, which will have to be supported by a deep transformation of business models. The transition from a fossil-based industry to a green one requires a process of technological and plant innovation, new skills, and a new, transversal working capacity.

The waste to chemicals technology makes it possible to combine two systems that have remained distinct until recently: Waste recovery and process industry. This integration generates a double advantage: The recovery of waste, converting it into secondary raw materials, and the transition from fossil to renewable sources. In the model for the Green Circular District, raw materials represent revenue and not cost, unlike conventional processes. Therefore, the marginal production cost (COP) from waste to chemicals using hydrogen, methanol, and ethanol is comparable to, and is even lower than, the marginal production cost from conventional systems. Table 1 lists the estimated production costs for ethanol, methanol, and hydrogen for given production capacities.

Table 1. Estimated production costs through the waste to chemicals process.

Chemicals	Waste to Chemicals COP	Conventional COP
Hydrogen	0.10-0.16 €/Nm³	0.06-0.120 €/Nm³
Methanol	260-400 €/ton	200-300 €/ton
Ethanol	400-580 €/ton	400-500 €/ton

Focus on circular hydrogen

One of the outcomes of the Green Circular District is "circular" hydrogen, which consists of low carbon produced through the recovery of carbon and hydrogen from waste using chemical conversion technology. Circular hydrogen is already an economically sustainable and workable transitional solution that facilitates decarbonization by recovering waste as a resource. Therefore, it can immediately launch the energy transition of a traditional, large industrial infrastructure. Hydrogen is the first element of the Periodic Table of Elements, and the most interesting: It is a building block, an energy carrier, has countless applications, and is present in the chemical formulas of any product. It is a full-fledged fuel that can be used for transportation. Plastic materials can be produced from hydrogen by adding the carbon and oxygen present in CO_2. Fertilizers, paints, and any other chemical or intermediate product can be created starting from hydrogen.

Hydrogen can support the decarbonization of highly energy-intensive sectors, such as the chemical and oil refinery industries, where it is already used as a raw material in the production of basic chemical products like ammonia and methanol (which we no longer produce in Italy), and in all refinery processes. Another sector where there is great potential is the steel industry, where hydrogen is the only low-emission alternative to carbon, both in the production of direct reduced iron (DRI) and in blast furnace production processes.

1.6. Concluding remarks

Building a Circular Green District represents an extremely interesting challenge, given the need to find synergy points between players in very different sectors, develop innovative and economically sustainable solutions to complex problems, attract investors, and ensure production capacity. The circular economy can be a key factor in rethinking the industrial infrastructure, creating work and long-term economic value. As demonstrated, the time is ripe, and it's also time to exploit the potential of economic theory for the revitalization and recovery of national economies. The Green Circular District can be the right tool, and it is in fact a solution to several problems, such as waste management, decarbonization of hard-to-abate sectors, and dependence on foreign imports of fossil fuels such as natural gas and chemicals. The Green Circular District is an example of how networking, joining skills, building alliances, raising awareness, and spreading knowledge about these issues can be an opportunity to build a sustainable and resilient future.

Industrial infrastructure rethinking, leveraging the circular economy, requires the help of the academic and university world, where students, who are our future thinkers (or re-thinkers), can learn how to identify and develop a Circular District and articulate their visions and contributions.

Part III

Chapter 1
THE CIRCULAR ECONOMY IN DELL RECONNECT

Pietro De Giovanni

ABSTRACT: *The Dell Reconnect program is a clear example of a how the circular economy aims at social development and inclusion through a tripartite of strategies consisting of reuse, refurbish, and recycle. Hence, this chapter explores the peculiarities of the circular economy implemented by Dell Reconnect, as well as all unexploited areas, such as the adoption of public funds and the use of digital technologies for smart circular economy systems.*

1.1. The e-waste framework

According to Kumar et al. (2017), e-waste can be considered any electrical or electronic equipment that someone discards when it reaches the end-of-life or end-of-use stage [1]. Since both of these categories are considered, the e-waste can include either working or broken items that are thrown away or donated to charity. Among the various product categories, e-waste can include home appliances (e.g., microwaves, home devices, electric cookers, and heaters), communication devices (e.g., cell phones, smartphones, laptops), entertainment devices (e.g., stereos, TVs, video games), electronic utilities (e.g., heating pads, remote controls, smart lights, monitors), and office and medical equipment (e.g., copiers, dialysis machines, defibrillators, blood pressure machines).

All of these product categories are subject to rapid technological obsolescence, which contributes to a growing amount of e-waste, even when products are not considered end-of-life or end-of-use goods. Incredibly, the technological waves are so quick and come with such unrelenting fre-

[1] Kumar, A., Holuszko, M., & Espinosa, D.C.R. (2017). E-waste: An overview on generation, collection, legislation and recycling practices. *Resources, Conservation and Recycling*, *122*, 32-42.

quency that many electronic devices still work fine when some consumer clusters consider them to be obsolete. Furthermore, these technological waves can drastically change the way consumers purchase and consume electronics. One clear example is VCR players, which have been replaced by DVD players, which were then in turn replaced by Blu-ray players. Hence, new versions and original releases of electronics contribute to the creation of e-waste.

These processes, in place for many years now, have induced consumers to purchase a lot of unwanted electronic devices, which have most likely been discarded in landfills. The US Environmental Protection Agency estimates that up to 60 million metric tons of e-waste end up in landfills every year[2]. These numbers scare all stakeholders within the electronics industry, because most electronics contain several forms of toxic materials such as beryllium, cadmium, and mercury, which seriously harm the environment and increase the risks of contamination of soil, water, air, and wildlife. Specifically, the e-waste can generate environmental problems like leaching, which consists of e-waste dissolving into microscopic pieces that remain in the ecosystem and cause traces of toxic materials to seep underground. Hence, e-waste induces metals and toxic materials to show up in the groundwater. In general, health risks may result from direct contact with toxic materials through leaching from e-waste. Minerals such as cadmium, chromium, brominated flame retardants, and polychlorinated biphenyls can significantly contaminate the environment and negatively affect people's health due to possible inhalation of the toxic fumes or the accumulation of chemicals in soil, water, and food. Indeed, such risks put people as well as land and sea animals in danger: The academic research has shown the detrimental effects of e-waste on individuals who work with the e-waste[3], and also the surrounding ecosystem[4].

While the urgency behind the problem of e-waste in landfills is evident and requires real action, there are other side effects to consider. One important motivation to avoid e-waste in landfills is the need for new sources of metal, an issue which has become very urgent in recent years, leading to the semiconductor crisis and breakdowns in many industries (e.g., automotive). Because of these difficulties, a proper circular economy strategy for e-waste is needed to protect the people, the environment, and future generations.

---

[2] https://www.epa.gov/international-cooperation/cleaning-electronic-waste-e-waste.

[3] Perkins, D.N., Drisse, M.N.B., Nxele, T., & Sly, P.D. (2014). E-waste: A Global Hazard. *Annals of Global Health*, *80*(4), 286-295.

[4] Grant, K., Goldizen, F.C., Sly, P.D., Brune, M.N., Neira, M., van den Berg, M., & Norman, R.E. (2013). Health consequences of exposure to e-waste: A systematic review. *The Lancet Global Health*, *1*(6), e350-e361.

1.2. The Dell Reconnect program

The Dell Reconnect program is a partnership between Dell and Goodwill agencies spread across the US, whose primary objective is to encourage the responsible and sustainable recycling of electronics. The main idea behind the Dell Reconnect program is that consumers can drop off their discarded electronics items – monitors, desktops, laptops, printers, scanners, keyboards, and more – at specified Goodwill kiosks across the US. The operators working in the Goodwill agencies evaluate each electronic item and decide whether to resell it as is, refurbish and then resell it, or recycle it. Upon returning their products, consumers receive a rebate that can later be used at their convenience (e.g., tax discounts), making the program economically appealing. When Goodwill displays used goods, both the used product and indifferent consumer segments are exposed to Goodwill's goods and prices. Therefore, it is imperative that Goodwill manage an important economic trade-off linked to the rebate: The rebate implies a considerable investment effort aimed at encouraging consumers to return their electronics. At the same time, it allows Goodwill to increase the return and, consequently, business opportunities and job creation, while lowering the amounts of electronics dispersed in the landfill.

1.3. Dell Reconnect and the waste cascade

The Dell Reconnect program seeks to focus on turning used electronics into recycling material, used products, and jobs. Each item arriving at a Goodwill location is inspected and analyzed to evaluate which of the waste cascade options should be undertaken. Specifically, the returned items can either be reused, refurbished, or recycled. *Reuse* means that a certain device or its components are in good condition and ready to be returned to work. *Refurbish* means that a device requires an upgrade or a slight modification before being returned to work; other components from other devices can be used to restore goods' capacity and performance. Once a device has been categorized as reusable or subject to refurbishing, it is cleaned and tested, such that it can be resold at one of Goodwill's stores. These options give people the opportunity to purchase devices at a great price, while new products of the same version are not affordable. Furthermore, these activities create new jobs for society, contributing to the social development and inclusion of some clusters.

When parts and devices cannot be reused or refurbished, they are subject to *recycling* activities, which consist of breaking them down securely and recycling them responsibly, such that all valuable material can be reprocessed to make new products. By implementing this tripartite strategy, the circular economy system adopted by Dell Reconnect enables the diversion of 1 billion pounds of e-waste every year from the landfill through 2019, which is equivalent to 2,000 jumbo jets, while fixing high-level targets from 2020 onward. Beside the environmental benefits, the circular economy system contributes to the purpose of Goodwill's agency goal, which is putting people back to work.

In principle, Dell Reconnect allows people to deliver any type of electronics, independent of its economic value and possible future usages. The waste cascade displayed in Figure 1 indicates that when devices are reusable or can be refurbished, their economic value is high, they reach the end-of-use stage, but they still have a way to go to the end of the life cycle. Therefore, the probability to extract value and benefit society is high. In contrast, electronics that are only recyclable are transformed into recycling material, which can either be sold to firms using it for their business or given to Dell as a counterpart of its contribution to the circular economy system.

Figure 1. Waste cascade for Dell Reconnect.

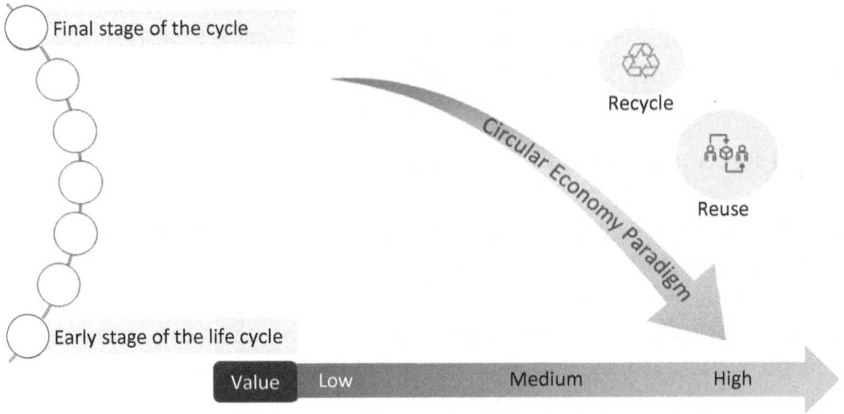

1.4. Users' engagement strategy for Dell Reconnect

One major issue that always emerges in the circular economy is the logistics strategy behind it. When goods must be collected around the ecosystem, the reverse logistics can be extremely challenging due to the high level of logistical costs. Reece and Norman (2006) have identified six main logistics cost categories[5] linked to the reverse flows:

[5] Reece, J. and Norman, L. (2006). The Six Hidden Costs of Reverse Logistics. In-

- *Labor*. Companies incur labor costs since their return processes are generally not automated. The only possibility of handling returns automatically is to implement a smart circular economy city.
- *Grey market items*. Firms can face the risk of returned items ending up on the grey market, where goods are sold outside normal distribution channels.
- *Lack of visibility*. Customers do not have access to return status information unless smart circular economy systems are implemented.
- *Inability to accurately forecast*. Firms need to implement ad-hoc forecasting algorithms to estimate the time, the quantity, and the value of returns in order to justify the economic viability of such return processes.
- *Credit reconciliation*. Large customers often calculate their own credits and take a debit on the next payment, which can be time consuming to reconcile.
- *Poor response time and brand toxicity*. Customers expect circular services during the entire life cycle, which make the services associated to the product costly and negatively affects brand value.

To avoid these emerging cost categories, the Dell Reconnect program has implemented an active return approach. Among the constellation of possible available mechanisms, Dell Reconnect identified the *tax discount* as the mechanism to be adopted for engaging consumers in activating the return process. Consumers bring their electronics to a Goodwill location; thereafter, following an inspection, the operators determine a tax discount rebate that consumers can use to secure a discount on their taxes during the next fiscal year. The amount of such an incentive depends on several features, including the weight of the electronics, the quality of the returns, their position in the waste cascade, and possible future return options.

Interestingly, the adoption of such an incentive mechanism allowed Dell Reconnect to make the reverse logistics strategy more efficient. The active return policy induces users to bring the unused electronics to the collection point; hence, the logistics strategy is no longer a problem since the goods are not supposed to be collected from the ecosystem while the users take an active part in the return process. Therefore, an active return approach allows Dell Reconnect to avoid the cost of manually handling returns, also avoiding the high capex linked to possible automation of the collection process. Furthermore, users enjoy visibility over the return process since they are the actors closing the loop of the circular economy, while the amplitude of the incentive can be adjusted to better control the return flow.

---

bound Logistics. Available at: https://www.inboundlogistics.com/cms/article/the-six-hidden-costs-of-reverse-logistics/.

For example, Goodwill can receive support from the government to increase user incentive during periods in which there is a scarcity of natural resources.

The incentives are also an important device to avoid costs related to credit reconciliation. Since consumers receive a tax discount option, they can simply conserve their tickets until the next tax declaration and use them to pay less taxes. Therefore, once the user leaves the Goodwill location with his or her discount in hand, the Goodwill agency is no longer responsible for the discount option. Finally, the incentive mechanism allows Dell to avoid complaints regarding delays in the circular economy service, since the latter is fully driven by users. Indeed, big companies like Dell organize reverse logistics activities in an optimized manner. In other words, they decide when and how to collect while optimizing the entire collection system. The solutions adopted by companies, although very robust and efficient from an operational and logistics perspective, can also cause users to be unhappy due to motivations such as delays in the collection process.

1.5. Emerging strategic consumer clusters

From a business perspective, the Dell Reconnect program benefits Dell by giving it more control over the second-hand market. While internet platforms like BestBuy.com allow consumers to purchase second-hand items, companies like Dell look at the second-hand market as a new competitor. Some consumer clusters are in fact exposed to second-hand electronics, even Dell-branded, over which original equipment manufacturers have no control. The presence of such atypical competition has led firms like Apple to manage end-of-use goods by implementing take-back programs, through which consumers obtain a rebate to be used for purchases of other goods of the same brand. Hence, the adoption of a take-back program has the objective of retaining consumers in the portfolio while acting on replacement strategies.

In contrast, the implementation of programs like Dell Reconnect does not force consumers to stick with a certain brand, as the rebate takes the form of a tax discount. In addition, Dell receives a great deal of social recognition, since the Dell Reconnect program leads to a better environment, the exploitation of minimal natural resources, minimal use of landfills, the creation of jobs, and development of the social community. Indeed, these benefits require Dell to rethink about the pricing strategies for new products as atypical challenges emerge[6]. On the one hand, prices for

---

[6] Ramani, V., & De Giovanni, P. (2017). A two-period model of product cannibali-

new products should be lower than the prices of competitors and affordable; this policy will give the signal that Dell strongly believes in social development and makes products available to the community. On the other hand, the low price for new products can entail the formation of new consumer clusters. In fact, knowing Dell's approach to prices and returns, consumers can become strategic and show three kinds of purchasing behavior: Consumers who always purchase new goods, consumers who always purchase used goods, and consumers who are indifferent with regard to purchasing either new or used electronics[7].

When Dell is challenged by pricing decisions with regard to new goods, which is appealing to consumers in both the new product segment and indifferent segments, the first cluster is indifferent to the presence of used goods in a Goodwill store, since they are always inclined to purchase new goods. Similarly, consumers purchasing used goods belong to a specific social cluster and have a social status that does not consent to the purchase of new goods. In this case, they always purchase used goods independent of any features. Then, the presence of indifferent consumers substantially challenges Dell. In fact, Dell and Goodwill compete to acquire consumers belonging to the indifferent segment, although the pricing strategies fixed by Dell for new electronics and the pricing strategies set by Goodwill for used goods differ. However, the pricing strategies that both firms establish also have a direct influence on their main markets. Therefore, some of the indifferent consumers can postpone the purchase of a Dell electronic device, with the hope that a used good will become available in a certain Goodwill store. Overall, although the Dell Reconnect program allows Dell to avoid atypical competition linked to the other sharing platforms, there are new cannibalization effects to consider, which require modern and unconventional forms of collaboration and agreements between involved stakeholders.

1.6. Circular economy coordination in Dell Reconnect

The scientific literature does not identify any type of coordination mechanism to be used when the circular economy project has environmental and social targets, as in the case of the Dell Reconnect program. The two major

zation in an atypical Closed-loop Supply Chain with endogenous returns: The case of DellReconnect. *European Journal of Operational Research*, 262(3), 1009-1027.

[7] Jalali, H., Ansaripoor, A., Ramani, V., & De Giovanni, P. (2021). Closed-loop supply chain models with coopetition options. *International Journal of Production Research*, 1-29.

entities, Dell and Goodwill, in addition to obtaining several informal benefits from the circular economy systems, such as brand enhancement, social inclusion, and environmental protection, could arrange a circular economy coordination mechanism to further develop the business model behind Dell Reconnect.

First, Dell can obtain exclusivity over the recycling material and purchase it according to a predetermined fee or a non-predetermined fee. In the former scenario, the companies require a signed agreement in which the fixed fee is identified, along with the unit of recycling material transferred, e.g., the tons of recycling material. This will lead to a very simple mechanism to transfer the recycling material, which allows Dell to avoid searching costs. In the latter scenario, the fee can be a function of some operational elements such as, for example, the quality of recycling.

Second, Dell Reconnect can adopt a revenue-sharing contract to coordinate circular economy activities, according to which for each unit resold into the secondary market in a Goodwill location, Dell receives a certain fraction of revenues. This can be either linked to products that are Dell-branded, which can eventually be covered by licensing or linked to all goods sold by Goodwill. Indeed, the two shares can be substantially different in considering the diverse quantity mobilized and the potential value of the recycling material.

1.7. Public funds available for the Dell Reconnect program

Considering the material and the information available, the Dell Reconnect program has been developed without requests for public incentives or available funds. However, considering the environmental and social impacts of such projects [8], public funds could be easily attracted and exploited in several directions. Among the public funds explored in this book, the following could surely apply:

- Promote the social economy through activities fostering the circular economy. These initiatives seek to promote social involvement in the collection, sorting, and repair of some specific waste streams in which Goodwill's operations can be reinforced and training programs can be implemented. Goodwill seeks to create social jobs by training operators in collecting, sorting, and repairing electronics, which require competencies and experience.

---

[8] De Giovanni, P., & Ramani, V. (2017). Product cannibalization and the effect of a service strategy. *Journal of the operational research society*, 1-17.

- Increase the guarantee periods. Dell can request these funds to extend the product life cycle by making goods more durable. However, this may contrast with the overall idea of the Dell Reconnect program; in fact, long life cycles imply low returns.
- Favor environmental labeling and certification. Dell Reconnect can request this funding to increase the visibility of its activities and stimulate purchases of used items from Goodwill stores.
- Communication about the repair of products. These funds could be used by Dell for new consumers to access content, by means of which the electronics can be easily repaired by users. Indeed, these funds will have the effect of extending the life usage of a good, operating against the purposes of Dell Reconnect. When these funds are used by Goodwill, they seek to make content available to second-hand users regarding how to maintain and repair electronics after the purchase.
- Low VAT on green products and services. The electronics sold at Goodwill locations may be subject to a lower VAT compared to the same products purchased new. This can influence people's sensitivity and willingness to purchase these products.

Indeed, these mechanisms could be used within the Dell Reconnect program as a single option or as a combined option, giving visibility to the program surrounding several aspects of the circular economy system.

1.8. Smart circular economy in Dell Reconnect

The Dell Reconnect program does not consider any digital technology within the circular system. However, future developments may yield several digital solutions. One of the most interesting digital applications may be blockchain technology. Today, most electronics are smart, and consequently, can continuously provide information to the ecosystem regarding their state, their use, conditions, time it was used, etc. These pieces of information can be all recorded on a blockchain platform and be made available to Goodwill as long as the electronics' technology reaches the location. In this way, operators have a larger batch of information available to determine whether a product can be reused, refurbished, or recycled. Since all information can be recorded on a blockchain platform, the estimations could be much more precise, and the operations could be carried out more effectively.

On the consumer side, access to all information recorded on the blockchain allows consumers to better determine whether an electronics product is in good condition, the residual life cycle, as well as the real potentialities.

Indeed, the presence of blockchain and the related smart circular economy system can be guaranteed when all components and related items within a certain product have been designed to be supported by blockchain technology. In fact, all elements of a system must interact with the blockchain. A new and atypical advantage can be gained by Dell Reconnect: All Dell-branded goods can be designed to be covered and supported by blockchain. In this way, consumers shopping for second-hand goods will be able to purchase Dell-branded electronics that are recorded on the blockchain, while other brands' electronics are not supported by blockchain. Indeed, considering the full information available for Dell's electronics, consumers may well prefer Dell products when making purchasing decisions.

Chapter 2

NEXTCHEM'S GREEN CIRCULAR DISTRICT MODEL

Pierroberto Folgiero

ABSTRACT: *In recent years, NextChem, a subsidiary of the Maire Tecnimont Group, has taken the lead in the environmental transition of the natural resources processing sector, focusing its capabilities on the development of technologies belonging to the green chemistry field. The Circular Green District model is the technological solution proposed by the company for the decarbonization of the industry through a circular economy. This chapter provides an overview of the technologies and the environmental benefits of the model.*

2.1. NextChem's Green Circular District Model

Maire Tecnimont S.p.A. is a company listed on the Milan Stock Exchange and is the parent company of an industrial group, a global leader in the supply of technology, engineering, and construction of large industrial plants for the transformation of natural resources (downstream hydrocarbon industry: Petrochemicals, fertilizers, as well as oil & gas refining). In recent years, Maire Tecnimont has focused its activities on its portfolio of technologies to address new market challenges, supporting the development and industrialization of an economy based on the use of renewable resources. NextChem is the Maire Tecnimont Group company that develops and manages technological initiatives to support green chemistry and the energy transition, with activities ranging from plastics and waste recycling to bioplastics and electrochemistry.

NextChem's portfolio includes proprietary and exclusively licensed technologies, technology integration platforms, and engineering, procurement, and construction (EPC) contracts. NextChem's industrial strategy is based on three development areas: Greening the Brown - technologies to reduce climate change and polluting emissions in existing, conventional plants; Circular Economy – technologies to recycle plastic waste and other waste materials, and; Green-Green – technologies that use residual vegetable or raw biological materials to make intermediates, biofuels, and bioplastics.

Thanks to its long-term experience in the realization of plants all over the world, Maire Tecnimont has a deep knowledge of the plastics and chemical markets. To offer concrete solutions for the production of low carbon plastics throughout their entire life cycle, it has implanted its expertise as chemical engineers in this new production chain. Given the deep knowledge of the specific characteristics and needs of polymers and chemicals to be used in the transformation chain in various industrial sectors, Maire Tecnimont is able to apply "reverse-engineering" to the process to better understand how to reproduce the same product using raw materials derived from the world of waste.

2.2. NextChem's technologies in Green Circular District

Upcycling, the first step in the Green Circular District model, refers to technologies that enable the mechanical recycling of post-consumer plastic waste. The result, following a subsequent "compounding" chemical treatment of the shaving (enhancement of the material via a process that improves its chemical and physical characteristic and ensuing extrusion into pellets), is the creation of high added value recycled polymers with the same properties as fossil-based plastic. This outcome bridges the quality gap between recycled plastic and virgin plastic, which means that these recycled polymers can be used for a wide variety of market applications. Therefore, the upcycling technology adds value to the finished product (hence the "up"). Unlike traditional mechanical recycling methods, this process generates recycled products with an elevated added value. Furthermore, upcycling is based on the so-called "reverse approach". Thanks to this technology's features, polymers can be created based on customers' specific requirements.

The process includes a careful polymer-wise and color-wise selection phase, followed by a volumetric reduction by crushing larger objects into flakes. Compounding is the extrusion phase, during which the flakes are extruded to obtain granulates. Upcycling technology used by NextChem under the MyReplast™ trademark[1] is installed on the plant located in Bedizzole, in the province of Brescia in Lombardy, managed by the

[1] In September 2020, NextChem registered the MyReplastTM trademark both for its proprietary technology upcycling and its product portfolio composed of recycled polymers.

NextChem subsidiary MyReplast Industries. The Bedizzole plant has a capacity of 40,000 tons per year and a recycling efficiency of 95%. The plant, with a total of 32,000 tons of plastic waste processed, reduced CO_2 emissions by 40,000 tons in 2020, compared to the same amount of plastics derived from oil. Upcycling gives plastic waste a second life, as secondary raw materials, and MyReplast™ products have received the EuCertPlast and Plastica Seconda Vita (Second Life Plastic) certifications[2].

We use plastic so often precisely because of its features, such as flexibility, reduced cost, and versatility. Meanwhile, the use of recycled plastic is less frequent, which is due to the deterioration of the material during recycling processes (Figure 1). MyReplast™ products are custom-made pellets and shavings created based on customers' specific needs and requirements: NextChem does not merely follow a "catalogue-based" approach. It also employs a "customer-based" approach to develop the final product alongside the customer, based on customized chemical and physical properties. Thanks to the combination of mechanical and chemical recycling, MyReplast™ technology facilitates the "design" of every feature of the materials, from the very start to the finished product.

Figure 1. MyReplast™ upcycling: Technological process and products.

[2] EuCertPlast is related to the process and certifies the quality management and traceability of a production site for certain product categories. Second Life Plastic certification is a product certification system for materials obtained from plastic waste sorting and industrial waste. It is the first Italian and European trademark dedicated to recycled plastics, which has adopted the concept of quality and traceability of recycled plastics.

2.3. Chemical Recycling

Waste that can be recovered via chemical recycling includes, for example, mixed plastic packaging from urban waste collection, refuse-derived fuels, and the so-called "dry fraction" of waste derived from the mechanical-biological treatment of mixed waste. Through a chemical conversion process, where hydrogen and carbon contained in this waste are recovered, a synthesis gas is obtained and can be used to produce compounds such as ammonia, methanol, ethanol, and hydrogen. Chemical recycling is a thermal process that differs from incineration, allowing the chemical conversion to happen via oxygen rather than by combustion. The process is known as "partial oxidation" and uses pure oxygen as an oxidizer. The conversion phase is followed by a subsequent purification phase, which prevents pollutants from being emitted into the atmosphere.

Therefore, the related gas can be considered "circular", as it derives from post-consumer materials that are recovered. The small quantity of CO_2 emitted during the process is compensated by the CO_2 savings due to not having incinerated the waste, which instead is recovered. The residues from the process are inert and can be reused in industrial applications such as, for example, brick making.

2.4. Process Description

The waste to chemicals process can be divided into three macro-phases:

- Waste chemical conversion
- Syngas washing and purification
- Syngas conditioning and final synthesis.

Phase 1 – Chemical Conversion

The carbon and hydrogen contained in plastic and dry waste are converted through a thermal process, which is different from combustion, into synthesis gas, as shown in the Figure 3. The process can be defined as "partial oxidation", and it uses the same waste as an energy source and pure oxygen as an oxidizing agent. The conversion phase is followed by a purification phase that prevents the emission of pollutants. The output gas can be considered "circular", as it comes from the recovered post-consumer materials. The CO_2 emitted during the process is offset by avoiding the incineration of recovered waste.

Syngas leaves the reactor at about 1100°C and is immediately cooled and brought to a temperature of 90°C to avoid the formation of dioxins. High temperature in the reactor is reached thanks to pure oxygen.

Figure 2. Reactor of the waste to chemicals process.

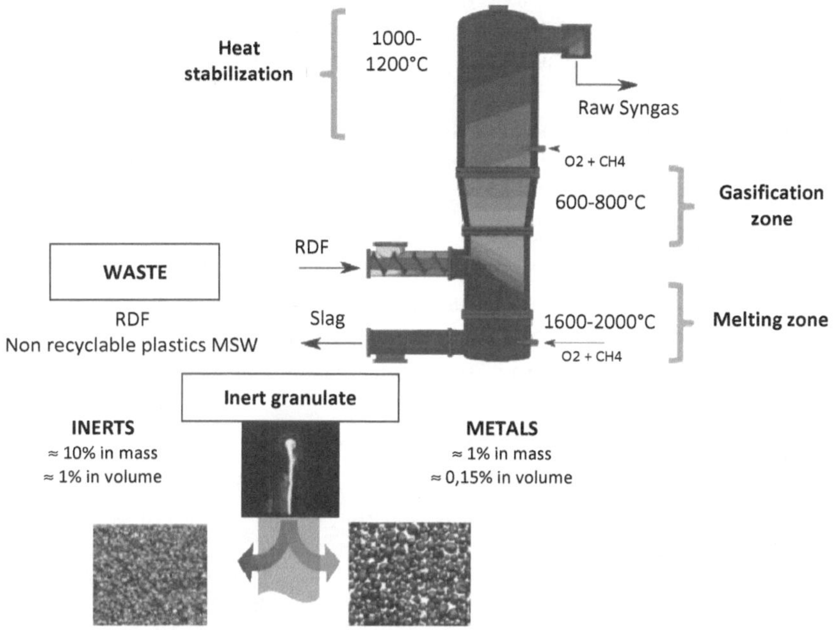

The lower section of the reactor has a temperature of at least 1600°C (Figure 3). This enables the melting of the inert waste fraction, which, once cooled, is collected as vitrified material without releasing harmful substances. The inert waste fractions (silicates, aluminates, metal oxides) are extracted in the liquid phase from the bottom of the reactor, free of organic fraction and vitrified by contact with water. It is worth noting that vitrification, which takes place after melting and organic fraction removal by high-temperature heating, is a part of the Best Available Technology (BAT) technologies used on waste to energy incinerators (both toxic and flammable) to produce inerts and reuse volatile ashes from the perspective of a full-scale circular economy. Therefore, the inert vitrified product can be used for civil and industrial purposes (rock wool, granulate for bitumen and cement, majolica, road surfaces, abrasive materials, and much more). Metals can be separated from the vitrified material and sent to steel mills. In a nutshell, the exploitation of synthesis gas and inert fractions enables a nearly complete conversion of waste into high-value products without resorting to landfills.

Phase 2 – Syngas

Once cooled, the syngas undergoes washing through a series of columns and filters that remove potential contaminants and particulates. Since the chemical composition of waste and its calorific value are naturally variable, syngas composition varies accordingly. To manage this "variability", a gasometer, among other countermeasures in this regard, is positioned between the purification and conditioning sections, to contribute to stabilization of the flow rate of the syngas to the downstream process units requiring a stable flowrate. The syngas is then further treated in the purification section. Once purified, it can be treated and converted.

Phase 3 – Conditioning and synthesis

Circular Gas can be used as is, thanks to its reducing qualities in hard-to-abate production processes, such as the steel industry, as a cheaper replacement of synthesis gas derived from methane or coal derivatives (such as carbon dust), thereby reducing greenhouse gas emissions.

Figure 3. Types of usage of synthetic gas, either for steel production processes or for refining processes.

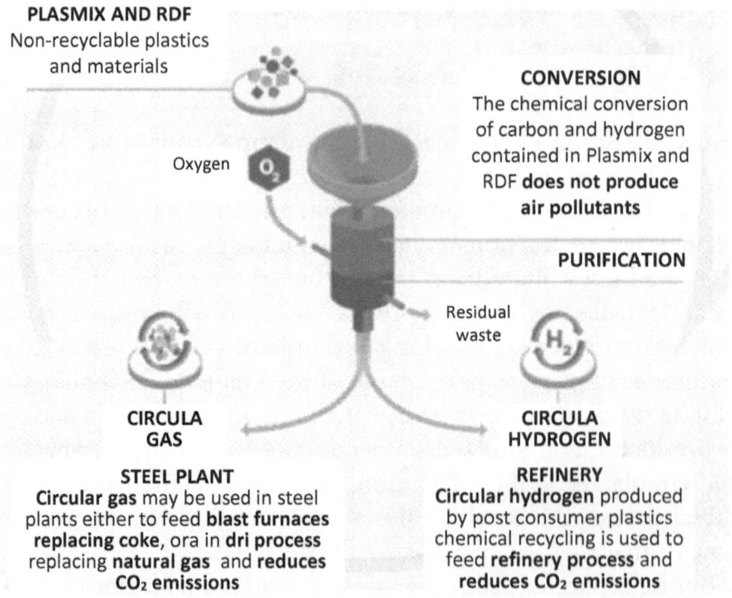

As shown in Figure 4, Circular Gas can also be used as a basis for the production of "circular hydrogen", methanol, ethanol, or a variety of other chemical compounds essential to industry. These products are used both as chemicals in many industries (for example, the furniture industry and sanitary products), and as low carbon fuels. The circular synthesis gas can be transformed into hydrogen, ammonia, methanol, ethanol (100% of the latter is currently imported from abroad by many European countries), and their derivatives.

Figure 4. Waste to chemicals products.

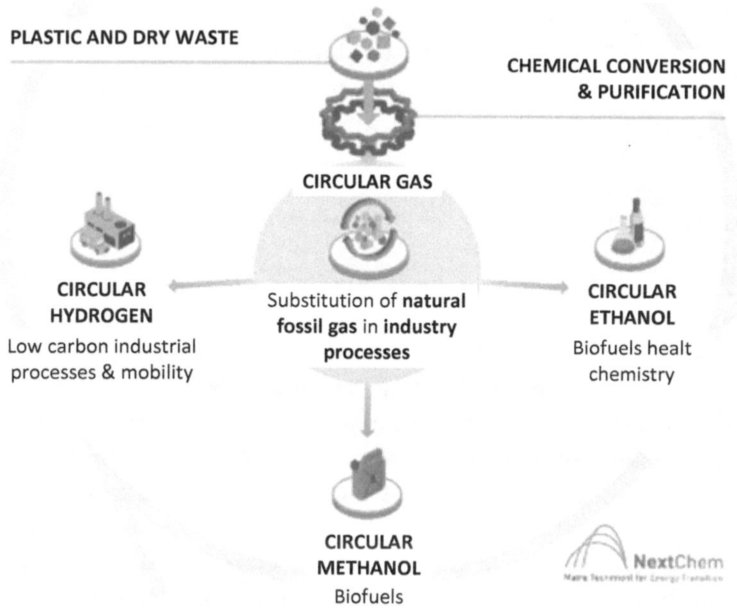

2.5. Circular hydrogen

To produce circular hydrogen, a stream of steam at 300°C is added to the output syngas. The mixture is then sent to two catalytic reactors, where the water gas shift reaction takes place[3]. The hydrogen is then separated per specific requirements in the separation system based on the alternating pressure conditions (Pressure Swing Adsorption[4]). After hydrogen separation, highly calorific residual gas, primarily composed of CO and CO_2, can be reused within the process, reducing the consumption of external methane and, therefore, emissions. The carbon contained in the residual gas

[3] Water-gas shift is a reaction producing hydrogen through the oxidation of carbon monoxide. The production of hydrogen occurs when an oxygen molecule passes from water to carbon.

[4] Pressure swing adsorption is used to separate certain gases from a gaseous mixture depending on the molecular characteristics and gas affinity to the adsorbent material.

separated from the hydrogen is recovered and used as an internal source of fuel.

Waste to hydrogen CO_2 savings

Steam reforming	*vs*	Waste to H_2 *minus* Landfill Waste

$$\text{SAVING } CO_2 = \frac{[CO_2 \text{ p. conventional}] - [CO_2 \text{ Waste to Chemicals} - CO_2 \text{ landfills}]}{[CO_2 \text{ p. conventional}]}$$

* SAVING CO_2= 80-90%

* Values for 192,000 tons of waste converted per year (expected composition 75% SRF, 25% mixed plastics), taken CO_2 emissions per MWh from European power grid.

To calculate the CO_2 savings, we need to consider the amount of CO_2 in a traditional steam reforming hydrogen producing system and subtract the CO_2 produced by waste to chemicals technology net of CO_2 that would have been produced if the waste used to produce hydrogen had been sent to landfills (avoided CO_2). The result is CO_2 saved, thanks to waste to chemicals hydrogen technology.

Electric power supply for industrial processes and mobility is among the guidelines set out by the European Commission to decarbonize industrial production. Waste chemical conversion proposed by NextChem is primarily based on the electric power supply at all stages. CO_2 emissions avoided, as reported in this document, depend on the emissions of the electric power source. This presentation shows the values linked to the national power source mix (about 30% of renewables). The trend line of increasing use of renewables to produce electricity shows a favorable CO_2 balance for the chemical conversion of waste.

Under ideal conditions of a 100% renewable power source mix, the above-mentioned values improve even further. We obtain a significant increase in savings for CO_2 (≥90%). Until today, the incineration of urban and hazardous waste has not been part of the CO_2 emissions reduction and monitoring system (ETS UE). However, since the guaranteed allowances are currently under discussion, one can expect that it will be gradually reduced to achieve carbon neutrality targets when new waste disposal technologies will demonstrate their ability to acquire significant market share at the expense of waste incineration.

In the case of CO_2, savings of waste chemicals exceed 100%, which can be considered carbon sink, as it extends beyond carbon neutrality by assuring a reduction in total emissions. Using waste to chemicals technology, 200 million Nm^3 (18,000 tons) of circular hydrogen can be produced from 192,000 tons of incoming waste per year[5].

2.6. Circular methanol

To make circular methanol, syngas must meet a certain stoichiometric ratio between H_2, CO and CO_2 molecules[6], which is called the methanol module (MM): $MM = (H_2 - CO_2) / (CO + CO_2)$. To guarantee this ratio and reduce consumption to a minimum, syngas is divided into two streams after the purification phase. One remains as is, while the other undergoes a conditioning process. The latter is first modified to increase the quantity of hydrogen using a high-temperature shift reactor, where the water is transformed into hydrogen and the CO is converted into CO_2. Then, to adjust the methanol modulus, the CO_2 is removed and recovered with a high degree of purity. At this point, the streams merge and are mixed with the hydrogen-rich stream coming from the pressure swing adsorption to reach the desired methanol modulus. The resulting syngas, which now meets the required stoichiometric ratio between the constituent molecules, is sent to the synthesis of methanol. The outgoing stream is separated, and the unconverted fraction is recirculated to the reactor to increase its energetic yield. A fraction is drawn from the recirculation stream to avoid the accumulation of inert compounds. This separated stream also feeds the pressure swing adsorption, which supplies the hydrogen stream.

Waste to methanol CO_2 savings

Fossil based methanol synthesis	*vs*	Waste to MeOh *minus* Landfill Waste

$$\text{SAVING } CO_2 = \frac{[CO_2 \textit{ p. conventional}] - [CO_2 \textit{ Waste to Chemicals} - CO_2 \textit{ landifills}]}{[CO_2 \textit{ p. conventional}]}$$

* SAVING CO_2= 80-90%

* Values for 192,000 tons of waste converted per year (expected composition 75% SRF, 25% mixed plastics), taken CO_2 emissions per MWh from European power grid.

Under ideal conditions of a 100% renewable power source mix, the

[5] All CO_2 savings data result from an internal assessment, and we are now considering applying for external certifications. 192,000 tons of waste is the standard volume of feedstock incoming to a typical plant.

[6] The quantitative ratio of chemicals in chemical reactions, i.e., the ratio of two or more chemicals reacting with each other.

above-mentioned values improve even further. NextChem obtains a significant increase of CO_2 savings (≥90%). To calculate the CO_2 savings, we need to consider the amount of CO_2 in a traditional steam reforming methanol producing system and subtract the CO_2 produced by waste to chemicals technology net of CO_2 that would have been produced if the waste had been sent to landfills (CO_2 avoided). The result is CO_2 saved, thanks to waste to chemicals methanol technology.

Using waste to chemicals technology, 100,000 tons of methanol can be produced from 192,000 tons of incoming waste per year[7].

2.7. Circular ethanol

Using LanzaTech syngas bacterial fermentation technology licensed to NextChem, ethanol is produced by bacteria, which transforms the Circular Gas at low temperature and low pressure, improving the entire sustainability of the process. Crude ethanol produced in the bioreactors is separated by distillation to a degree of purity fit for conventional applications. The circular ethanol resulting from this process can be mixed with gasoline, replacing fossil components and achieving a lower carbon footprint. When made from dry waste containing non-fossil fractions (e.g., wood), 40% of the circular ethanol can be considered "advanced" according to the European Renewable Energy Directive[8].

Therefore, waste to ethanol technology consists of a chemical conversion process (with the know-how provided by NextChem) aimed at the production of syngas. Finally, the fermentation process seeks to transform the syngas into ethanol (know-how is licensed by LanzaTech on the Italian market).

Waste to ethanol CO_2 savings

Fossil based gasoline	*vs*	Waste to Ethanol *minus* Landfill Waste

$$\text{SAVING } CO_2 \; \frac{[CO_2\ p.\ conventional] - [CO_2\ Waste\ to\ Chemicals - CO_2\ landfills]}{[CO_2\ p.\ conventional]}$$

* SAVING CO_2= 75-85%

* Values for 192,000 tons of waste converted per year (expected composition 75% SRF, 25% mixed plastics), taken CO_2 emissions per MWh from European power grid.

---

[7] All CO_2 savings data result from an internal assessment, and we are now considering applying for external certifications. 192,000 tons of waste is the standard volume of feedstock incoming to a typical plant.

[8] Directive (EU) 2018/2001.

To calculate the CO_2 savings, we need to consider the amount of CO_2 in a traditional gasoline producing system (ethanol may replace various components used in gasoline production) and subtract the CO_2 produced by waste to chemicals technology net of CO_2 that would have been produced if the waste had been sent to landfills (CO_2 avoided). The result is CO_2 saved, thanks to waste to chemicals ethanol technology.

Under ideal conditions of a 100% renewable power source mix, the above-mentioned values improve even further. NextChem obtains a significant increase of CO_2 savings (≥90%).Using waste to chemicals technology, 62,000 tons of ethanol can be obtained from 192,000 tons of incoming waste per year [9].

2.8. Waste to Chemicals vs Incineration

Compared to incineration, waste to chemicals technology offers a number of important benefits in waste management, first and foremost of which is a waste volume reduction from 1:5 of an incinerator to 1:100. It is a technology designed to maximize the production of CO and H_2 and convert the carbon contained in the waste to produce syngas. The synthesis gas produced by waste using waste to chemicals technology is not directly emitted into the atmosphere, as it is subsequently converted into hydrogen, methanol, and ethanol. In addition, the inert granulate can be reused in civil industry, while the bottom residue from an incinerator consists of flammable and toxic volatile dust that must be disposed of in landfills.

The differences in terms of environmental impact between incineration and chemical recycling are shown in the table below [10].

---

[9] All CO_2 savings data result from an internal assessment, and we are now considering applying for external certifications. 192,000 tons of waste is the standard volume of feedstock incoming to a typical plant.

[10] The data are the result of an internal assessment.

Table 1. Differences between waste to chemicals and incinerator.

INCINERATOR	CHEMICAL CONVERTER
Designed to maximize CO_2 and H_2O production.	Designed to maximize CO and H_2 (syngas) production.
Almost all of the carbon from the waste goes to CO_2; the remaining fraction comes out as bottom ashes.	The carbon from the waste is partially or totally converted into a new chemical product.
The bottom residue contains carbon and appears as flammable and toxic volatile dust. It is disposed of in landfills and can cause toxic eluate.	The bottom residue is an inert granulate that can be used in the civil industry, to recover metals or produce rock wool.
Uses considerable air excess. The combustion of solid materials is difficult to control.	Works under controlled flow rates of pure O_2, which guarantees greater control of the temperature and the process.
The fumes require careful abatement. Potential releases of dioxins, furans, particulates, and NOx, in particular during transient modes.	Clean gas can be used for the synthesis of chemicals, fuels, or energy production, so it is not emitted into the atmosphere.
The sulfur contained in the waste is converted into sulfur oxides and released into the fumes, potential hazards of acid rains.	The sulfur in the waste is converted to H_2S is recovered as elemental sulfur to be sold on the market.
Waste volume reduction 1:5.	Waste volume reduction 1:100.
High consumption of natural gas to ensure full combustion.	Low consumption of natural gas to control thermal profile.

2.9. Green hydrogen production by electrolysis

The Green Circular District model also enables electrolysis technology to convert electrical energy into chemical energy. Electrical energy converts the water molecule (H_2O) into H_2 and O_2 using electrochemical processes. If electrolysis is powered by renewable energy sources, the hydrogen produced is defined as green, i.e., the most sustainable form of hydrogen, with zero CO_2 emissions.

Green hydrogen, if produced electrically from renewable sources, becomes a very low emission fuel and a raw material for the production of further low-emission chemical products. Water molecule splitting into its two basic elements, hydrogen (H_2) and (oxygen) O_2, is enabled by two electrodes, a cathode, and an anode, where hydrogen and oxygen are released, respectively. These two gases are separated inside the electrolyzer by membranes and diaphragms integrated into the machine and are then sent to a water washing system and subsequent dehydration system. After that, both gases are compressed and ready for their final use. Using electrolyzer and renewable energy as power and water as feedstock, the production of green hydrogen does not cause any CO_2 emissions.

Potentially, renewable hydrogen represents one of the most flexible carbon-neutral energy carriers, with the greatest potential for development and utilization in various sectors such as energy, mobility, heating, and industrial decarbonization, where it can be used as a source of both thermal energy and raw material.

If electrolysis is integrated into a Green Circular District, the injection of renewable hydrogen into the waste to chemicals process increases its yield. It helps capture CO_2, improves the conversion of carbon into high added value products, and is capable of replacing fossil alternatives.

Furthermore, it is also possible to exploit and recover the oxygen co-produced by the electrolyzer and use it inside the conversion units to further increase the efficiency of the system and obtain a 100% circular solution.

Thanks to the integration of the green waste to chemicals and fuels hydrogen production via electrolysis in a Green Circular District, the carbon footprint will be further reduced, and the yields of the chemicals produced will improve by 80%, optimizing the entire process. An example related to methanol production: By adding green hydrogen to the system and considering it as a natural complement to the waste to chemicals technology, having the same input feedstock, the related circular methanol can increase from 110,000 to 200,000 tons per year.

INDEX